The History of Arizona

Robert Woznicki, Ph.D.

The History of Arizona

ISBN 0-9618094-3-4 $15.95
6th Edition

Published by:
Woznicki Publications
925 E. Broadmor Dr.
Tempe, AZ 85282
(480) 967-1287 FAX (480) 966-6852
email: doctorrwoz@aol.com

Cover Design by Cheryl Gorder
Blue Bird Publishing

Cover Photo of interior of Bank One Ballpark
provided by Arizona Diamondbanks

Publishing Services Provided By:
BLUE BIRD PUBLISHING
1916 W. Baseline #16 Mesa AZ 85202
(480) 831-6063 FAX (480) 831-6728
Email: bluebird@bluebird1.com
Web site: http://www.bluebird1.com

Table of Contents

Dedication

To my brother, Marshall, who gained tremendous success in the business world, the old-fashioned way--

He earned it by hard work, self-sacrifice and diligence.

Acknowledgments

The Author wishes to thank the Arizona Office of Tourism and Marshall Trimble for their pictures as well as the Diamondbacks Media Guide for information on Jerry Colangelo and the new ballpark. Kudos are to be given also to Cheryl Gorder, the owner of Blue Bird Publishing, who helped immensely and was an excellent consultant.

About the Author

*Robert Woznicki, M.A., M.A., Ph.D., is best known
as an Arizona History lecturer and author. His other
titles are Madame Curie, The History of Yuma and
the Territorial Prison, A Current Analysis of International Education, and 2 volumes on world history.
He was on the faculties of many high schools and
junior colleges in Arizona. He was an instructor for
the Dependent School Program with the USAF
schools in Libya, Spain and England. In Asuncion,
Paraguay, he was the Director of the Central Cultural School. He also was on the faculties of the University of Maryland, San Diego State University, the
University of Warsaw, Poland, Beijing University
Post and Communications and the Beijing Second
Language Institute in China. He has done research
at the Universities of Oxford and Cambridge in England. In Michigan, he was Superintendent of Schools
in Marne. Presently he is Adjunct Professor of History for Northern Arizona University in Flagstaff.*

Introduction

My mattress was spread always upon the ground, with a buffalo robe under it and a hair lariat around it, to keep off the snakes; as it is said they do not like to cross them. I found the ground more comfortable than the camp cots which were used by some of the officers, and most of the women. The only Indians we had seen were the peaceful tribes of the Yumas, Cocopahs and Mojaves, who lived along the Colorado. We had not yet entered the land of the dread Apaches.

Martha Summerhayes
from *Vanished Arizona 1865*

Mother Nature and man have seldom given to the world in one breathtaking package, such a panoramic view of beauty on this earth, from prehistoric to the modern age, as the State of Arizona.

Arizona's great canyons and sunken deserts, her bold buttes and strange eroded rocks, her painted sands and petrified forests are nature's masterpieces. They are a record of the world's creation.

Only yesterday cowboys with colts and lariats rode their horses down these streets where today automobiles roll. Before that, cliff men, fighting with spears, peopled these mountains while the valleys are fragrant with orange and grapefruit blossoms. This is a land where the ever present cactus is in the desert. It is a land of open spaces and dust storms.

New frontiers have always been new horizons of hope. Arizona very well fits this description. It has always been a new frontier and for thousands of people who have gone to Arizona and many who still come, it is a land of hope, of new adventure, of a different style of life.

The name Arizona brings to mind extremes and paradoxes in both geography and climate. Just as Arizona's geography is grand and diverse, so is her history. The record of man in Arizona offers the historian a subject matter of dimension and significance, equal to that of a sovereign nation. As one great historian wrote of Arizona, no other American state would, if isolated, be so truly a great and magnificent nation in itself.

Arizona's development has been influenced by all manner of people—explorers, Indians, Padres, trappers, traders, whalers, miners, cattlemen, cowboys, politicians and farmers. A history of Arizona must first do justice to her Indian beginnings and then to the long years of Spanish and Mexican jurisdiction which contributed so much to the shaping of her past and present. It must describe and analyze the main changes brought by Arizona's American era, changes that become increasingly dramatic in the twentieth century.

Arizona and its surrounding territory has always had a reputation as a place of drama in pioneer days. It was a sort of frontier beyond the frontier. In the summer it was God's forsaken place. This was the American Sahara and, except for the northern part of the state, where it was cooler, few cared to live here. It called for a special vocation to live in such a torrid area. In its early history few came to Arizona and very few stayed.

There were really no trees, no grass, no shrubs in many parts of the State. In much of the area there was only the monotonous sands of the desert and the ever present sun. There were always the deadly windstorms of the desert which threatened to cover the hovels of the tiny village with dunes. Plants of the desert were green only immediately after rains, which were few and far between.

In this wasteland then years ago, death was ever present. It was arid and desolate. Many died from lack of water on various journeys to and from Arizona. The curse of the Grim Reaper was always behind you. Deadly snakes, the Gila monsters, ta-

7

rantulas, etc., all took their toll.

But the winters in Arizona are the most delightful in America. Only Egypt has a comparable climate. Arizona is a wonderful place for the old and the young in the winter seasons.

The question could be asked, and it is an academic one: Why should anyone want to come and live in Arizona in the old days? The answer can be given by saying that these pathfinders had what we call the PIONEER SPIRIT. This was the passion that made America and it made her great. Such were the pioneers who with great courage settled Arizona and made it the fabulous state that it is.

Arizona has come a long way since 1864 when J. Ross Browne wrote about Arizona in his *Adventure in the Apache Country:*

> No country that I have yet visited presents as many striking anomalies as Arizona. With millions of acres of the finest arable lands, there was not at the time of our visit, a single farm under cultivation in the Territory; with the richest gold and silver mines, paper money is the common currency; with forts innumerable, there is scarcely any protection to life and property; with extensive pastures, there is little or no stock; with the finest roads, traveling is beset with difficulties; with rivers through every valley, a stranger may die of thirst. . . . In January one enjoys the luxury of a bath as under a tropical sun, and sleeps under double blankets at night. There are towns without inhabitants, and deserts extensively populated; vegetation where there is no soil, and soil where there is no vegetation.

Snow is seen where it is never seen to fall, and ice forms where it never snows. There are Indians who are the most docile in North America, yet travelers are murdered daily by Indians, the most barbarous on earth. The Mexicans have driven the Papagos from their southern homes, and now seek protection from the Apaches in the Papago villages . . . Mines without miners and forts without soldiers are common. Politicians without policy, traders without trade, storekeepers without stores, teamsters without teams, and all without means, form the mass of the white population.

STATE OF ARIZONA

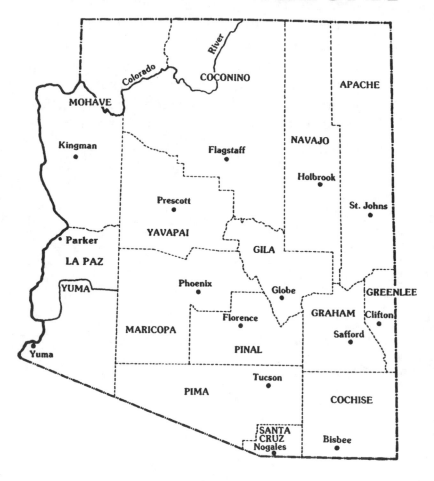

ARIZONA COUNTIES
AND
COUNTY SEATS

Chapter One

SOME INTERESTING FACTS ABOUT ARIZONA

An embarrassing oversight delayed the opening of the forerunner of Arizona State University at Tempe. It seems that in the rush to construct someone forgot to erect outhouses for the students and faculty. The error was discovered just two days prior to the opening of school and a special meeting was called to remedy the situation. A committee of one board member, Charles Trumbull Hayden, saw to it that the proper facilities were added and the first term in 1866 opened on schedule.

Marshall Trimble
from his book, *Arizona*

1. One of the oldest cities in the United States is the small village of Oraibi, Arizona, located in Navajo County near the city of Winslow. It is believed to have been in existence since the fourteenth century. Once the largest of the Hopi towns, its population of 800 at the turn of the century was reduced to about half in 1907, when many of the people left to found the village of Hotevilla, seven miles west.
2. As early as 1866 women teachers in the school system of Tempe had to abide by these rules:
   1. No smoking or use of spirits.
   2. Marriage or other unseemly behavior was not to be tolerated.

11

3. Joining of any feminist movement, such as the Suffragettes, was forbidden.

As late as 1915, the women teachers found their lot almost as bad with these rules:
1. Women may not dye their hair.
2. Two petticoats must be worn.
3. You are not to keep company with men.
4. You may not loiter downtown in ice cream stores.
5. Dresses must be two inches above the ankle.
6. You may not dress in bright colors.

3. Whoever heard of Arizona having a navy? Well, it did. In 1934 California utility companies were battling Arizona for water rights to the Colorado River. Governor Moeur of Arizona at that time sent two patrol boats, the Julia B and the Nellie T, to cruise the Colorado River to make sure that all would be aware that Arizona was determined to protect her rights. As it turned out, the two boats and members of the national guard got tangled in weeds and cable, and had to be towed by their adversaries. Arizona's navy was disgraced.

4. Arizona had been known for its cowboys and its cactus. But no one would identify Arizona with ostriches. Yet into Phoenix they came around the year 1885. Women demanded them for their hats and it became a flourishing business in the Valley of the Sun for quite some time. They required less water than cattle, and they were profitable. The industry lasted to about 1916 when women decided that ostrich feathers were no longer in style.

5. Arizona has the largest nuclear plant in the United States—Palo Verde—located about 55 miles west of Phoenix. The plant has three large units. The domed structure that houses the reactor contains 7,100 tons of steel rods and 40,000 cubic yards of cement.. Investing in the $6 billion project are the Arizona Public Service, Salt River Project and utilities in California, New Mexico and Texas.

6. On July 3, 1887, the first train rolled into Phoenix. The Maricopa and Phoenix Railroad Company offered the town only a branch line that connected via Tempe, with the main line of the Southern Pacific Railroad at Maricopa. Phoenix had about 3,000 people at that time. Besides some private investors, Maricopa County, as authorized by the territorial legislature, subsidized the line to the tune of $200,000.

7. The first American mining boom in Arizona was in the Tubac area. Silver mines were developed there by Mexican laborers working for Sylvester Mowry and Charles Poston ("the Father of Arizona"), and other well known pioneer entrepreneurs.

8. The first man to hold a Cabinet rank from Arizona was Stewart L. Udall who was Secretary of the Interior under President John F. Kennedy. Arizona has two lawyers who have been appointed to the Supreme Court: Chief Justice William Rehnquist and Sandra Day O'Connor, who was the first woman in our nation to hold this office. Both are considered to hold very conservative ideology.

9. Many historians speculate as to where the word "Arizona" came from. Most say that is came from two Spanish words: Ari (da) zona. Others say it takes its name from a small settlement on a rough road near the border called, in 1730, La Real de Arizona.

10. Near the southern border of the state, Arizona has a preserve of cactus that cannot be found any other place in the United States. The Organ Pipe Cactus National Monument is an unspoiled desert wilderness, where 330,000 acres flourish, mostly filled with sundry kinds of cacti.

11. During the Second World War, two Japanese-American relocation camps were situated in Arizona. One was at Poston and the other was at the Gila River Indian Reservation. These Japanese-Americans were being placed in the camps upon orders signed by President Franklin Delano Roosevelt in

1942. Most of the Japanese were from the West Coast area.

12. Green Valley, Arizona, is a very well known retirement community located about halfway between Nogales and Tucson. Founded in 1964, it is a successful, modern city of about 25,000 residents. One must be at least 55 years of age to buy a residence.

13. There is a Strawberry, Arizona. It is a small community about 110 miles northeast of Phoenix, with an elevation of 6,047 feet.

14. Arizona is famous for its major league baseball teams which come here in the spring before the official season begins. Known as the Cactus League, such teams as the Chicago Cubs, Oakland Athletics, San Francisco Giants, San Diego Padres, California Angels, Seattle Mariners, Colorado Rockies and the Milwaukee Brewers attract thousands of baseball fans.

15. In 1864 Charles Debrille Poston, the first Indian Superintendent for Arizona, selected the area known today as the Colorado River Indian Reservation. The reservation, established on March 3, 1865, is alive with historic and prehistoric archaeological wonders. A mastodon skull, estimated to be forty thousand years old, was recently discovered on the reservation.

16. Arizona's most famous Indian trading post is located in the village of Ganado. Hubbell's Trading Post is still operating as it has been for nearly a century. It has been designated a National Historic Site.

17. Located adjacent to the tribal administration building of the Kaibab Paiute Indian Reservation in Northern Arizona, is the famous Pipe Springs National Monument. It was established in 1932 to preserve the outstanding works of the early Mormon pioneers.

18. Perhaps one of the richest reservations in the United States is the Salt River Indian Reservation, located in eastern

Maricopa County immediately adjacent to Scottsdale, Mesa and the metropolitan area of Phoenix. The 49,000 acre reservation was created by an Executive Order of June 14, 1879, for the Pima and Maricopa Indian tribes who have inhabited the area for centuries. Scottsdale Community College is located on leased reservation land.

19. The Salt River Canyon, often referred to as the mini-Grand Canyon, is a chasm through five hundred million years of geological history, easily viewed along U.S. Highway 60 which follows and crosses the canyon.

20. The celebrated Superstition Mountains are located about forty miles east of Arizona State University. Many people, challenged by the thought of discovering the "Lost Dutchmans's Gold Mine," still search the mountains for its location. The name of the mountains, of which Superstition Peak at 5,057 feet is the highest, can be attributed to the legends of the nearby Pima Indians.

21. Mining in Arizona is not confined to gold, silver and copper. From 1900 to 1945 there was commercial production of mercury from the mines near Sunflower. The remains of these mines are visible from the Beeline Highway en route to Payson. The Iron King Mine near Humboldt was for many years a major producer of lead zinc.

22. Franciscan records of July 4, 1776, tell of explorers' supplies being left at the Yuma Indian village of Alvadore Palma. The explorers were packing much of what today's picnickers choose: beans, beef, cheese, biscuits, ham and chocolate.

23. In 1870, seven Sisters of St. Joseph of Carondelet braved dust, Indian attacks and proposals from woman-hungry men, to establish the Sisters' Convent and Academy for females in Tucson.

24. Arizona has many outstanding people of Polish extraction who have made their talents known in Arizona. Among them

are Frank Gordon, Chief Justice of the State Supreme Court; Frank Kush, head football coach at Arizona State University; James Ernest, the noted trumpeter of the Big Band era; Dr. Ted Zakrzewski, the well known cardiologist; and Dr. Robert Woznicki Jr., a noted psychiatrist.

25. The extreme northeast corner of Arizona marks the only place in the United States where four states meet. The Four Corners, as they are known, are made up of the following states: Utah, Colorado, New Mexico and Arizona.

26. Sylvester Herrera was the state's only winner of the Congressional Medal of Honor in World War II. Fred Ferguson, United States Army helicopter pilot, won the Congressional Medal of Honor in the Vietnam War.

27. The summers in Yuma are known for their intense heat as the summer thermometer often hovers near 120 degrees. The story is told of the reckless sinner who passed on and went down to his unfortunate punishment. When he got here, he sent back for his blankets. It was cooler there than in Yuma.

28. Ice was first manufactured in Phoenix in 1879. In 1880 the medical service industry was initiated in Arizona with the building of St. Mary's Hospital in Tucson, the only hospital in the state at that time. The first public rodeo in the United States was held in Prescott in 1888. The first telephone system was established in Phoenix in 1892 by the Sunset Telephone and Telegraph Company.

29. One of Arizona's best-known characteristics is that it is a state mostly owned or managed by the federal government. Of its 114,000 square miles, only about 15 percent (17,000 miles) is in private hands. The remainder is made up of federal forests, wilderness, parks, Indian reservations and military installations. It is quite obvious that Arizona has a very small tax base, and that its politicians for years have been battling the federal government, which tries to dominate policy in this state.

30. No history of Arizona can be written without paying tribute to the contributions of the Mormons. Many came from the Salt Lake City, Utah, area and they played a big role in the development of this state. Many Mormons are to be found in cities like Thatcher, Show Low, St. Johns, Safford and Mesa. The author has had many Mormon students in his long career as a professor and will tell you they were always well behaved and highly motivated.

Chapter Two

SYMBOLS OF ARIZONA

Arizona is blessed with a panoramic beauty that almost defies description. Only a limited number of poets, painters, and photographers have been able to do justice to her splendor.
Marshall Trimble

Arizona stretches north to south about four hundred miles while the east to west width is about three hundred thirty-five miles. Altogether Arizona, the nation's sixth largest state in area, contains 113,956 square miles, of which about 145 are water. The northern part of the state is a land of high mountains and plateaus streaked by deep, penetrating canyons and snow in the winter season. Near Flagstaff, Humphrey's Peak tops all elevations at 12,670 feet high. In the high plateau region is the fabulous Grand Canyon, one of the seven wonders of the world. It has an average vertical depth of one mile. One cannot really describe the pure and awesome beauty of this region. Almost 4-1/2 million people now live in Arizona.

The southern part of the state centers around the well known cities of Tucson and Phoenix. Most people know these areas for their heat and cactus. This is desert country and when one travels to the city of Yuma, one knows what the Sahara must be like in the summertime. But the glorious winter weather of these celebrated resort towns has made Arizona famous. Yet even in this land of the coyote and the Gila monster, everything is not the same arid type of topography. An hour's drive out of Tucson, for example, will take you from saguaro-like desert to cool forests atop the famous Mount Lemmon. Truly Arizona is a state of amazing variations of climate and topography.

We have learned from archaeological studies at the Ventana Cave, northwest of Tucson, that living humans were in the Arizona area some 20,000 years ago. And from the studies of various Indian tribes, as well as excavations at Casa Grande, Tuzigoot and Kinishba, we have learned that Arizona indeed had early residents going years and years into the past.

Arizona has a number of symbols of statehood. Let us begin with the state flag.

The Arizona state flag represents the copper star or Arizona rising from a blue field in the face of the setting sun. Old gold and blue are the colors of the state. The blue is the same shade as that of the flag of the United States. The lower half of the flag is a blue field while the upper half is divided into thirteen equal segments of rays which start at the center and continue to the edges of the flag, consisting of six yellow and seven red rays. A five-pointed copper star, symbolic of the state's enormous copper industry, is superimposed on the center of the flag.

The state flower is a blossom of the saguaro cactus, the largest cactus found in the United States. The saguaro (sah-war-oh), or giant cactus (carnagia gigantes), is found in Arizona and Northern Mexico with a very few scattered along the Colorado River in California. This cactus grows to a height of fifty feet, and lives to an age of 150 to 200 years. Its pure, white, waxy flowers appear in garlands on the tips of the long arms of the plant in May and June.

Arizona's state bird, the cactus wren, is a true lover of

the desert country. The wren's nests in cactus plants are common. The more thorny plants serve as protection. A woody-brown bird, with a speckled breast, he will build not one, but several nests, using one as a home and the others as decoys from his enemies. Nesting time for the cactus wren begins as early as March and extends into June.

The twenty-first Arizona State Legislature, second regular session, designated the palo verde (geus Cercidium) as Arizona's state tree. The palo verde (from the Spanish meaning green stick or green pole) is one of the beautiful trees of the desert. When it blossoms, generally in April or May, depending on elevation, it is a blaze of shimmering, yellow gold. There are two native species of palo verde ceridium in Arizona: the blue palo verde, characterized by a blue-green color of the branches and leaves; and the foothill palo verde characterized by the yellow-green color of branches and leaves. Both bear a profusion of yellow blossoms when in bloom.

But the greatest symbol is the Grand Canyon. God shed his light on Arizona when he created this popular tourist attraction. It is a broad intricately sculptured chasm that contains between its outer walls many colorful peaks, buttes, and canyons. It ranges in width from 4 to 18 miles and in length about 217 miles. The deepest and most impressively beautiful section, 56 miles long, is within Grand Canyon National Park, through which the Colorado River winds for 105 miles. At 8,200 feet above sea level, the North Rim is 1,200 feet higher than the South Rim.

The first sighting of the Grand Canyon is credited to the Coronado expedition of 1540 and subsequent discovery by Garcia Lopez de Cardenas.

Grand Canyon National Park, containing 673,575 acres, was created in 1919. Many pueblo and cliff dweller ruins, with accompanying artifacts, indicate prehistoric occupation. There are about five Indian tribes living on nearby reservations.

Other symbols of a lesser degree would be the Kachina doll, the cowboys and Indians who played such an important role in the saga of this state, the beauties of the desert, the Arabian horses which are raised here, the fantastic weather which attracts millions of tourists each year, the Indian jewelry that is worn by millions all over the world and the Arizona State University football team which played in the Rose Bowl on January 1, 1987, and defeated the University of Michigan 22-15.

Another museum of great interest can be visited by going north on Highway 17 about 25 miles from Phoenix to Pioneer, Arizona. Here is a living history museum of great note recalling the 1870s-1890s of Arizona legends. It is the largest museum west of the Mississippi. Pioneer features buildings moved from original sites from all over Arizona. The furniture is all western and the working personnel all wear western clothes dating back to the 1890s. Many school children visit there and guided tours teach these youngsters the realities of the golden West of the past.

Chapter Three

SPANISH MISSIONS DOMINATE ARIZONA HISTORY

Passing very near it, we entered upon the more than forty leagues of coast and new road between there and the mouth of the Rio Grande (Gila) and its confluence with the Rio Colorado. By the natives whom we found along the road, we were received with all love. We spent the 22nd of February, the day of the Chair of St. Peter in Antioch, on the Rio Grande, where more than fifty native, Pima, Yumas, Opas, and Cocomaricopas, had gathered. We named the pass and rancheria San Pedro and another rancheria nearby was named San Pablo.

Eusebio Franscisco Kino S.J.
in *Memoirs of Pimeria Alta,*
February 7, 1699.

Located in Arizona, the "baby state" of the United States, are Spanish missions surrounded by legends, history and strong religious convictions, all of which have had vital roles in the development of the territory of Arizona.

When the Spaniards first came into Southern Arizona during the seventeenth century to establish the mission of San Xavier, they visited the Indian village of Bac, the site which

22

today is Tucson, oldest and second largest city in the state. The mission was named San Xavier del Bac because of the nearby village.

The group of Spanish settlers, headed by Father Eusebio Francisco Kino, discovered that most of the villages of the Hohokam culture were in ruins—dwellings occupied at the time were dome-shaped mud and brush huts, rectangular mud and brush houses or open-sided shelters. Thus, the first work of the Spanish missionaries was to teach the Indians to make adobe brick by churning a mixture of mud and straw with their bare feet, forming blocks by hand and setting them in the sun to bake. The Indians were encouraged to build new homes with their new adobe bricks around the new mission.

Father Kino's Spanish priests also taught the Indians the fundamentals of irrigation and farming. San Xavier's founder recorded that on the grounds of the mission he grew wheat, maize, grapes, figs, oranges and melons—crops which the Papagos continue to raise on their nearby farms. The Spanish are also credited with having been the first to teach the Indians to grind their maize with grinding stones, one of the old fashioned methods still used by Arizona tribes.

San Xavier's church is the only one of the early Spanish churches now in use, the remaining twelve other mission established by Father Kino and his followers were deserted years ago and left in ruins.

Now a landmark of the tide of the Spanish Conquest, the ruins at Tumacacori, located eighteen miles north of Nogales, have been made a National Monument under the supervision of the National Park Service. The mission was established late in the seventeenth century and, like San Xavier, was founded by Jesuit Padre Kino. Tumacacori was one of the chain of Catholic missions founded by the Spanish extending from Mexico to California.

The church at the Tumacacori Mission was built by the

Indian followers of the Spaniards and was constructed with sun-dried adobe bricks laid in mud mortar. Though generally typical of mission architecture, the rectangular shaped church at Tumacacori, with its massive square corner tower and superimposed columns, suggests the earlier and more classic traditions established in Spain by Juan de Herrera. More than fifty feet wide and one hundred feet long, the church has black and red pebbles imbedded in the mortar on the north wall.

Adjacent to the church, forming a hollow square, were priests' residences which show evidence of having been small, comfortable dwellings. Located on the east side of the church was an oblong building where metallurgical operations were carried on. At the present time remains of furnaces and quantities of slag attest the purpose of the building.

The church building at Tumacacori, which today is under the jurisdiction of National Park Service employees, was dedicated in 1822, but abandoned a few years later when the Franciscans were expelled from Mexico shortly after Mexico won her independence from Spain.

Father Kino's birth date is not known, but is believed by historians to have been about 1640. Before accepting priestly orders he had acquired a reputation known as the Great Apostle to the Pimas. He became a priest because he believed he had been restored to health from a dangerous illness through the intervention of St. Francis Xavier, and he determined to devote his life to the conversion of the heathen in America. He added Francisco to his name, which became Eusebio Francisco Quino, afterward changed to Kino.

The keeper of a very detailed diary, Father Kino recorded for future generations accounts of his hardships and accomplishments in establishing the Arizona missions. It is through the records passed down by the padre that Arizonans have come to know the history surrounding the founding of the early missions.

Arizona has a large percentage of Indians. The leading tribes are the Pima, the Apaches, the Navajos, the Hopi, the Maricopa and the Papago. It was for these tribes that the Spanish first built the missions in Arizona and whom the early priests converted. They also were the ones to use the missions as garrisons during their wars—the towers at Tumacacori served as lookouts for the Apaches on numerous occasions. Even now the congregation at San Xavier is composed mostly of Papago Indians.

Today the stately white mission buildings at San Xavier and the ruins of the Tumacacori Mission are two of the main attractions in Arizona.

Historians say that thirteen missions and rancherias were at one time established in the territory which today comprise the State of Arizona; however, many of these missions were in existence only a short while, some having closed in 1736 when Father Ignacio Keller visited the territory. One of the early missions, San Miguel de Guevavi, was named for the Indian village, Guevavi, which has disappeared from modern maps. The mission was established by Father Kino and Father Juan Maria de Salvatierra who had a large Indian following. The Sobahpuris Indians, who lived at Guevavi and were responsible for the founding of the mission there, traveled two hundred miles to find the padres and ask them to come and establish their mission. The continuing interest in the Catholic faith by Arizonans is evidenced in the fact that over fifty percent of the state's population today is Catholic.

Among the earlier missions were Immaculate Conception and St. Andrew, both of which were established by Father Kino. The physical buildings of the missions have not been preserved. Sonoitac, another of the early Arizona missions, was deserted around 1784.

The mission of San Augustine del Tucson was founded in 1769 by Father Garces, a Franciscan monk. Father Garces was a leader in the early mission work and it was he who made Tucson a walled city. He was killed in 1781 by the Indians in Yuma.

Established in villages forming a chain from Mexico City to the Pacific Coast, the majority of the early missions are to-day connected by a modern west coast highway popularly known as "El Camino Real".

In general the Arizona missions all followed the same building pattern. The churches, which dominated the grounds of the missions, were rectangular buildings. There were some few exceptions in the mission chain, notably the San Xavier church which was cruciform.

The architecture of the early Spanish fathers used for their shrines during the seventeenth century has been handed down through the history of Arizona. Many of the modern schools of the state are in various ways duplicates of the mission buildings. The adobe brick, first made by the Indians under the supervision of the Spaniards, is used for modern Arizona municipal buildings and homes.

As the Pilgrims were landing at Plymouth Rock in the eastern United States, the Spanish padres were advancing into the western territory of Arizona. They left behind them an indelible impression which even today dominates the religion, architecture and customs of Arizona.

When Mexico gained its independence from Spain in 1821, the new government decided to break up the mission system. The congress in Mexico City made all Spanish clergy take an oath of loyalty to the new government. All foreign missionaries were sent back to their homeland. Because the philosophy of the Mexican government was anti-Spanish, the missions slowly disappeared. In 1834 the Mexican government began to sell the mission lands. In 1844 the mission land near the famous church of Tumacacori, Arizona, was sold at public auction for $500.

Chapter Four

SCENIC WONDERS

The first missionaries who viewed the Grand Canyon described it as one of God's finest creations. The modern cynic might mutter acidly that it looks like a bad case of soil erosion, while a cowboy might gaze into its vast abyss respectfully and quietly observe that is would be a "hell of a place to lose a cow."
Marshall Trimble
in his book, *Arizona*

Just southeast of the Grand Canyon National Park lies another of nature's wonders— the Painted Desert.

The Painted Desert extends for three hundred miles along the north band of the Little Colorado River. Eons of rain and wind have exposed the highly-colored shales, marls and sandstones. Warm, almost unreal tints waver across the sands, dance along the mesa tops, stain the lomas and ledges and splash scarlet hues from horizon to horizon. The caprices of heat, light and desert dust frequently change the colors from blue, amethyst and saffron to russet, lilac and blood red. At times even the air above this lonely land glows with a pink mist or a purple haze. In the early morning and evening the mesa seems to broaden. Mountains a hundred miles away rise in clear profile.

In one of the most colorful sections of the Painted Desert is Dinosaur Canyon. Here, in the canyons and on the cliffs, have been uncovered over three hundred dinosaur tracks, the largest number ever found anywhere in the world. The largest track measures twenty inches in length. The imprints were probably left there at least 40,000,000 years ago. The trip to Dinosaur Canyon in late afternoon when the setting sun sets fire to the red cliffs is one of the memorable occasions in a lifetime.

The Painted Desert was included in 1936 as an addition to the Petrified Forest National Monument—one of Arizona's superb national masterpieces. This National Monument, which covers 90,302 acres, also takes in much territory south of the Painted Desert region and contains altogether six separate forests of petrified wood. This area was a low-lying swamp basin in Triassic time, 160,000,000 years ago and the trees floated in by streams flowing from the surrounding highlands. The logs were then buried by stream deposits and by volcanic ash. While buried, the wood of the logs was replaced by the mineral silica, or quartz, carried in solution by ground waters. Iron oxide and other minerals stained the silica to form the present rainbow colors. Later the region was uplifted and the action of wind and rain removed the covering sediments to expose the logs.

Of the six forests, Rainbow Forest is the largest and best known. Many of the trunks are more than one hundred feet in width. The outer sections are usually reddish brown, but the cross sections reveal every tint of the rainbow. Some have been reduced by the elements into piles of chipped agate, onyx, carnelian and jasper.

An Indian legend tells of a goddess, hungry, cold, and exhausted, who was pleased when she found hundreds of logs lying on the ground. She killed a rabbit with a club, expecting to cook it. But the logs were too wet to burn. Enraged, she cursed the spot, turning the logs to stone so they could never burn.

In this same broad circle of great natural sights, north of the Petrified Forest National Monument and northwest of the Grand Canyon, lies Monument Valley. This valley is famous for outcrops of red sandstone, several hundred feet high, which have been eroded into pillars and spires or into huge rectangular blocks with grooved sides suggesting columns. From a distance these rose-colored rock monuments, looming above the desert, have the aspect of the ruins of gigantic Greek temples.

Historically this valley is interesting, having been at one time the home of the Navajo Indians. When Kit Carson rounded up this tribe in Canyon de Chelly in 1863-64, Chief Hoskinnin led his people into this area, where he lived in complete independence till his death in 1909.

Monument Valley has its legend of hidden treasure. In 1880 two men named Merrick and Mitchell made a prospecting trip into the valley and returned with quantities of almost pure silver. From their second trip neither returned. They were found shot. Mitchell Butte and Merrick Butte are the natural monuments to the two men.

We pass over other great natural wonders in Arizona which are chiefly geologic records of past ages. These include: the natural bridges, among them Rainbow Bridge, so called from its rainbow arch; Sunset Crater, the almost perfectly preserved crater of an extinct volcano; and El Morro National Monument, the great butte monolith resembling a fort on the old road followed by the Spanish conquistadores of the seventeenth and early eighteenth centuries and bearing inscriptions of their travels.

We come now to nature's living miracles in the form of the giant cacti in Saguaro National Monument, in the southwestern part of the state. This monument, seventeen miles east of Tucson, is a tract of more than 63,000 acres containing a forest of twenty-six species of cacti, the greatest of them, the saguaro. These corrugated giants with their perpendicular branches look more like the strange dreams of a modern artist than living growths. Many of them are more than one hundred years old and have attained a height of fifty feet. They are a comparatively rare species, as their habitat is limited to southern Arizona and northern Mexico. The saguaro's ability to store water against the dry season is remarkable. Water absorbed during the rainy season is sucked into the trunk, which expands its spine-covered accordion pleats to serve as a reservoir. A mature plant may take up as much as a ton of water following a soaking rain.

In spring the saguaro bears waxy, white blossoms at the ends of its branches. These develop in late June into purple fruit which is a favorite food of the Papago and Pima Indians. Its harvesting is the occasion for a Papago festival. The Indians eat the juicy red pulp, both fresh and sun-dried, and boil the juice into a syrup that is very intoxicating when allowed to ferment. The ripe fruits furnish food, too, for several varieties of birds, particularly the whitewinged dove, and for small mammals such as chipmunks and ground squirrels.

The giant cacti provide nesting sites for many kinds of birds including the gilded flicker, the Gila woodpecker and desert wren. Other wildlife seen in the Saguaro National Monument include mule deer, wild hogs, coyotes, badgers, rabbits and foxes.

As for other forms of vegetation, in April and May, the desert is yellow with the bloom of the palo verde and mesquite trees; while hillsides are aflame with the red flowers of the ocotillo.

Of equal interest with Arizona's magnificent geological spectacles are its archaeological sights. The state is covered with the remains of early civilizations. Arizona has been the home of hair aborigines who stoned to death the giant sloth, the mammoth and many other beasts now extinct. It has been the home of nomads who sheltered in natural caves, hunted with spears and bows, yet developed the art of basketry to a high point. Cliff dwellers who built homes of stone and shaped clay into pottery lived here. Likewise pastoral tribes who built pueblos and planted corn and cotton beside irrigation canals left their mark here.

Important among the archaeological treasure spots in the Grand Canyon State is the Canyon de Chelly National Monument in Northeastern Arizona, within the Navajo Indian Reservation. This monument covers 83,840 acres and includes Canyon de Chelly and Canyon del Muerto.

The walls of the sandstone canyons rise to heights of 700 to 1,000 feet. In natural crevices in their sides are many cliff-dwellers ruins. Perhaps the most famous is the White House Pueblo, which was occupied for 200 years in about 1060 to 1275.

In the one national monument can be seen the development of ancient southwestern civilizations, with but few periods lacking.

More recent history credits the Spanish with entering the Canyon de Chelly and fighting with the Navajos of this region in the early nineteenth century. Later in 1863-64, it was the scene of Kit Carson's greatest feat when he campaigned all through this canyon, rounded up 7,000 Navajos and exiled them to New Mexico in their final defeat. The difficulties were described in a report of 1864, which said:

> This is the first time any troops have been able to pass through the Canyon de Chelly, which, for its great depth, its length, its perpendicular walls, and its labyrinth character, has been regarded by eminent geologists as the most remarkable upon the face of the globe. It has been the great fortress of the tribe since time began. To this point they fled when pressed by our troops. Many military commanders have made an attempt to go through it, but had to retrace their

steps. It was reserved for Colonel Carson to be the first to succeed.

About 500 Navajos live along the canyon bottoms, where the water can be utilized for irrigation.

Montezuma Castle National Monument in the Verde Valley of central Arizona protects another group of these cliff dwellings, among the best preserved ruins in the Southwest. Montezuma Castle, a five-story, twenty-room structure, is the best of these cliff homes which honey-comb a limestone cliff bordering Beaver Creek. With its foundation nearly 50 feet above the cliff base, the castle is reached by a series of ladders, and is 40 feet high. It is remarkably well-preserved owning to the fact that it is protected by the overhanging cliff.

Near the castle are many smaller structures of from one to five rooms. Some three hundred to three hundred fifty persons probably had their homes in these prehistoric apartment houses, which were occupied from the eleventh to the fourteenth centuries.

The sedentary farmers who occupied this fertile valley were driven to take shelter from marauding warlike tribes in their high rock niches. The visitors can picture some keen-eyed sentinel discovering enemies on the far horizon and then warning all the farmers working in the fields below by thumping on a huge tom-tom.

In 1694 the Spanish missionary, Father Eusebio Francisco Kino, discovered a large ruin on the Gila River which he named Casa Grande. At that time the ruins must have been standing in much the same condition that they are today, except that a large cement roof has been built over them for protection.

The Casa Grande is located in Casa National Monument, 67 miles north of Tucson. It was erected more than eight hundred years ago as a watchtower by the prehistoric farmers who lived in the six villages which are included in the reservation.

It stands four stories in its center room and three stories in its four outside rooms, the walls rising about forty feet above the desert level.

It is believed that the Casa Grande people, called the Hohokam Indians, were originally nomads who came to the Valley about 2,000 years ago. They settled here and developed an irrigation system, the ruins of which are still seen. The Hohokams left records of their civilization, including pottery, finely engraved necklaces, rings, bracelets and bangles of shell.

Other important records of prehistoric man are found at Navajo National Monument, which contains remarkable thirteenth-century pueblo cliff dwellings and at Tonto National Monument, which has fourteenth-century Pueblo cliff homes. Altogether, there are probably 100,000 of these prehistoric ruins in Arizona.

Chapter Five

A LOOK AT HISTORY

Tucson is cursed by the presence of two or three hundred of the most infamous scoundrels it is possible to conceive. Innocent and unoffending men were shot down or bowie-knifed merely for the pleasure of witnessing the death agonies. Men walked the streets with double barreled shotguns, hunting each other as sportsmen hunt for game. In the graveyard there were 47 graves of white men in 1860, and of that number only 2 died natural deaths.

John C. Cremony, 1860.

Many think of Arizona and its past in terms of cowboys fighting Indians. Many young people watching a John Wayne movie or a late TV scenario have the image of Arizona as the Wild West. The old and the young just think of Arizona as dusty and full of western towns which have saloons and cowboys— and maybe an honest sheriff or two. The period of the cowboy and Indian lasted only a short time in Arizona history, 1850-1886. Actually it was a small part of a saga that is rich with people, various cultures, violence and wars and a panorama of events unparalleled in the development of any of the fifty states.

In 1528 a Spanish explorer named Alvar Cabeza de Vaca landed in what is now Florida with an exploring party. They were attacked by Indians and all were killed but Cabeza de Vaca, two other Spaniards and a big black man called Estevan. The Indians took them captive. Cabeza soon convinced them of his abilities as a medicine man and they allowed him and his followers to go about as they pleased. They were not given their full freedom, however, until one day they met some Conquistadores coming north from Mexico. These were the first Europeans they had seen in years. Cabeza de Vaca was to return with them to Mexico City, where he told all about the seven fabled cities of gold and his years with the Indians. He had mastered the Indians language and probably knew more about their culture than any man alive with European blood at that time. He excited all Mexico City about the gold and many wanted to return and look for it in the land of the north called Pimeria Alta.

The viceroy of Mexico, Mendoza, now sent Fray Marcos de Niza with some Indian servants, and the black man, Estevan, to seek the gold. Father Marcos sent Estevan and some of the Indians ahead. If the land was good, Estevan was to send back two small sticks in the form of a cross. The better the land, the larger the cross was to be. Imagine Father Marcos' surprise when a short time later two Indians appeared carrying a cross as large as they were. He was delighted and hurried after the Indian guides hoping to catch up with Estevan. When they arrived at the San Pedro River in what is now Arizona, they found some of the camp sites used by Estevan. Sad to say, they were to learn that Estevan had been killed by hostile Indians.

The Indian guides were frightened and did not want to proceed, but Fray Marcos persuaded them to go on for a few more days. Finally, one evening, they could see a "city" in the distance. Perhaps to the Indians a village of some 200 huts seemed large. But one wonders how Fray de Marcos could have been mistaken. And mistaken he was, for he was to report that this was the first of the seven cities of gold. Perhaps the tiny flakes of mica in the adobe walls glinted in the rays of the setting sun, and made the city look like it was golden. After all it was twilight and the human eye does deceive itself at this time of the day. At any rate the loquacious Fray de Marcos returned to Mexico City and told all that he had seen one of the golden cities.

Three hundred soldiers led by Francisco Vasquez de Coronado, hundreds of Indian slaves and several priests made up the new expedition. They had horses, cattle, sheep, hogs, goats and many pack animals. Their expedition was to cost about two million dollars. They must have been an exciting sight as they started out; the Conquistadores in their silks and fine armor, the long robed priests, the foot soldiers, Indian slaves, pack animals and finally the animals being herded along.

They sent some of their supplies by two ships up the Gulf of California. The ship's captain, named Alarcon, and his men found the mouth of the Colorado River and sailed north on it until it became too shallow for the ships. He is said to be the first European to see the present site of Yuma, Arizona.

Coronado and his men came as far as northern Arizona but found only small villages. They conquered some of these and took the available food but they found no gold. One of the soldiers found the Hopi villages. The Hopis were a peaceful tribe. They soon made friends with the Spaniards, and told them of a large river west of the villages. One Spaniard, Captain Garcia de Cardenas, went to investigate and returned and told Coronado that the river was useless to them as it was at the bottom of a mile deep canyon. He had discovered the famous Grand Canyon on the Colorado River.

Finally, in 1542, after several years of unsuccessful searching, the remnants of the expedition returned to Mexico City, ragged and empty-handed. Poor Fray de Marcos was blamed for their failures and he sadly returned to Spain.

Forty years went by, then another Spaniard, Antonio de Espejo, and Fray Bernardina Beltran returned to Arizona and discovered silver in the Prescott area. Others followed and mining began in Central Arizona, but the Indians were hostile and the mines were so far from Mexico that working them was not very profitable.

At last the Spanish Padres, who were Jesuit priests, came and with engineering skills acquired from their advanced culture began to build a chain of missions which changed the complexion of the West. They brought knowledge of farming and medicine and totally upgraded the life of the Indians. Many of these Indians converted to Catholicism, for the Jesuits were excellent teachers.

Later in 1768, the Franciscan Fathers, another group of Roman Catholic priests, made their way into the pages of Arizona history. Fray Francisco Garces came and made San Xavier his headquarters. He wanted to establish a trail between these and the missions in Southern California where another Franciscan, Father Junipero Serra, held a monumental reputation as the Father of the California Missions.

Life in southern Arizona flourished even though some marauding bands of Indians occasionally raided the mission communities and stole the livestock. There were no huge problems as long as the Spanish soldiers held sway in the area.

When the struggle for Mexican independence began and was finally won, the Spanish soldiers were naturally withdrawn. Mines were abandoned and people fled to Tubac or Tucson to escape from Indian raids.

Until 1848, all of Arizona was a part of Mexico. Then in the treaty of Guadalupe Hidalgo, the United States gained all the land north of the Gila River. Later the Gadsden Purchase of 1853 acquired the rest of what is now Arizona. It must be remembered that for two hundred years the Spaniards held Arizona and the Southwest. Spanish courtesy and sense of leisure, fiestas, rodeos, etc., have all influenced Arizona's progress and culture.

During the Civil War, Arizona was in sympathy with the South. Many residents at the beginning of the Civil War were from the South. Shortly after hostilities began, the federal government pulled all troops out of the area to fight in the East. Moreover, the United States government issued a new mail contract to the Butterfield Overland Stage Company, permitting it to bypass Arizona to the north. This event caused many Arizonans to feel as if the government in Washington had abandoned them. Without the protection of U.S. troops, the mining and ranching activities of the area came to a standstill. Many were left to face the warring Indian tribes with really nothing but their own guns to protect them.

On August 1, 1861, Lieutenant-Colonel John R. Baylor and three hundred Texans seized Mesilla, New Mexico, in the name of the Confederacy. Mesilla was named the Confederate capital of the Southern Territory of New Mexico, which included all of Arizona and New Mexico, south of the 34th parallel from the Rio Grande to the Pacific Ocean. The only Civil War battle to be fought in Arizona took place near the town of Red Rock at Picacho Pass. Actually it was more of a skirmish than a battle, with twelve Northern troops, led by Lieutenant Jack Swilling. The North suffered six casualties: three dead, including Lieutenant Barrett, and three wounded. The Southern force had two wounded and three captured. The Northern victory marked the beginning of a strategic withdrawal of Confederate forces from Arizona.

Even though full records are not available in some instances, Arizona Indian groups at one time or another, to a greater or lesser degree, fought the Spanish, Mexicans or Anglo-Americans in an effort to maintain their cultural identities. Small, impoverished and isolated tribes, such as the Cocopah,

Havasupai, Paiutes and Hopi were left alone and, as a result, had little or no conflict. But the fight and ferocity of the Apache is well known. For almost a quarter of a century and the expenditure of many millions of dollars, the American, the Apache and many other tribes fought each other and thousands of lives were lost.

In 1860 Arizona was a county of the New Mexico Territory with a total population of 6,482 according to the U.S. Census. This census lists only 2,442 of these as "Whites" and the rest "Indians". Undoubtedly there were many more Indians in Arizona county than 4,040. These 4,040 must have been only Indians who lived in or near communities and military establishments and who had peaceful commerce with the early settlers, traders and soldiers.

The communities listed in the Census of 1860 were eight in number. This was the complete list, regardless of size, of all non-Indian settlements in Arizona. Tucson (pop. 915) is the only one of the eight that has maintained a prominent role. The others were: Gila City (pop. 150); San Xavier (pop. 200, of which 35 were "White"); Tubac (pop. 353, of which 310 were "White"); Patagonia (pop. 5); Ft. Mohave (pop. 130); Ft. Bachanan (pop. 142); and Maricopa Wells (pop. 53).

Arizona Territory was formed February 24, 1863, from the western part of the New Mexico Territory. The newly-formed territory had four counties: Mohave, Pima, Yavapai and Yuma. Pah-Ute County was created from the northern part of Mohave County in December 1865, but most of this county (12,225 square miles) was given to the State of Nevada in 1866. The remaining portion was returned to Mohave County.

A special Territorial Census was conducted in 1864. At that time the non-Indian population numbered 4,573. According to the U.S. Census of 1870, the territory's population had grown to 9,658. The Arizona list of communities with population over 100 had grown to fourteen. Only four of these had been listed in the 1860 census: Tucson, Tubac, San Xavier and Mohave City. Pima County of 1870 included part of present-day Pinal County so that the then new towns of Florence and Adamsville were listed in Pima County.

When Arizona became a territory, Camp Whipple in Yavapai County was established as an Advance Army Post. Governor Goodwin said that the territorial capital should be near Ft. Whipple. Prescott came into existence in 1864 and soon was the capital of Arizona Territory.

The decade from 1870 to 1880 was a period of great growth for the Arizona Territory. Its 1880 population of 40,440 was over 300 percent greater than its 1870 population. Much of this population growth had occurred in the last few years of the decade, concurrent with the advance of the two great railroads across the south and across the north of Arizona.

Arizona now was beginning to settle down into a modern culture. The last of the Apache troubles was settled in 1886. Permanent settlers and traders soon followed the miners to the rich silver discoveries, such as Globe and Tombstone, and established communities. The members of the Church of Jesus Christ of Latter-Day Saints (Mormon) established colonies along the Little Colorado River and later penetrated deeper into Arizona, creating permanent agricultural centers.

Shortly after the railroads were completed, a price war between the two railroads did even more to populate the West. In 1885 many people who wanted to move west but could not afford the regular fare, jumped at the chance to migrate at reduced rates. The two companies realized that neither could freeze out the other and stabilized fares at a price of $50. This was a great bargain and helped to bring about the greatest western immigration since the Gold Rush Days. The majority of these immigrants went to California, but many stopped in Arizona or returned when they found California unsatisfactory.

By 1890 three more counties had been established, making a total of ten counties. The population of Arizona had grown to 88,243—a ten-year increase of 118 percent. There were 35 cities and towns having a population of over one hundred in the 1890 census of Arizona. It represented 15 newly reported towns and the dropping of 17 towns which had been listed in the 1880 census. The new towns appeared in mining areas where new discoveries had occurred, in cattle raising areas where the addition of railroads and the quelling of Apache Indian terror had benefited cattle raising and along the northern route of the railroad. Of the 17 communities dropped, 12 were mining communities that died when the rich ore ran out, three were abandoned military posts and two (Brigham City and Ehrenberg) were affected by the meandering of Arizona's rivers.

Many diverse factors affected economic growth during the 1890 decade. Early in the 1890s torrential rains flooded grazing lands and washed away topsoil. Resulting damage to range lands brought about heavy cattle losses. However, income derived from the industries of citrus production on a commercial basis, and the increased gold production resulting from the invention of the cyanide process for extracting gold from ore, tended to offset losses experienced in the cattle raising industry. The national financial panic in 1893 brought about devaluation of silver and the subsequent closing of many silver mines. The following year use of new processes for extracting copper revived the mining activity. Also during this decade, three major fires swept Jerome—the first in 1894, the second in 1898 and the third in 1899. It seems significant to note that the first long staple cotton was planted in 1899, a crop that has contributed greatly to the Arizona economy over the years.

The first decade of the twentieth century saw great growth in mining areas such as Globe, Jerome and Bisbee, and considerable growth in cities along the railroads such as Winslow, Willcox and Yuma. Copper production and development boomed throughout most of the first twenty-five years of the century, spurred on both by the demands of war industry and by improved technological processes. Some of the most notable occurrences from 1900 to 1910 include: the great Prescott fire in 1900, the railroad spur line to Grand Canyon in 1901, the incorporation of Salt River Valley Water Users Association in 1903 and its signing of the agreement to build Roosevelt Dam the following year, the forming of the Miami Copper Co. in 1906, the first large scale production from low-grade copper ores at Morenci in the same year, the prohibition of gambling in 1907 and the establishment of the Grand Canyon as a national monument in 1908.

By 1910 Arizona's population had reached 205,354, an increase of 66 percent over 1900.

During the decade of 1910 to 1920, population continued to gain. The completion of Roosevelt Dam in 1911 and the subsequent availability of irrigation water greatly expanded agricultural development throughout the Salt River Valley. Later, dams and irrigation facilities on the Salt River and Verde River made it possible to open thousands of acres for cultivation. In 1910 the people of Arizona were pushing for statehood. The State Constitutional Convention was held in this year and the new State Constitution was ratified early the next year. Though Congress approved Arizona's constitution in 1911, President Taft vetoed admission until certain amendments were made. On February 14, 1912, Arizona was formally proclaimed the 48th State of the Union. Statehood did much to attract new pioneers and to develop all facets of the former territory.

One of Arizona's pioneer luxury resorts, the San Marcos Hotel, built in 1910 in Chandler, was the forerunner of many luxury winter resorts to come to central and southern Arizona. The Camelback Inn and Mountain Shadows Resort, both in Paradise Valley, are others.

Roosevelt Dam was dedicated on March 18, 1911. It was to supply the water for the future growth of metropolitan

Phoenix.

The first large scale copper flotation process plant in the United States was built in Inspiration.

In 1919, the State's first commercial aviation company was formed in Tucson.

By 1920 the population had grown to 334,162—a 63 percent increase during the preceding ten years. The impetus gained during the war carried into the first year of the new decade, but the postwar depression had a dampening effect on Arizona's fabulous growth in population, industry, commerce and agriculture. Phoenix College was established in 1920 and the state Legislature passed the state's first Workmen's Compensation Act in that year. In 1924 the Southwestern National Monuments Office was created to protect and administer some of the scenic and historical monuments.

Toward the middle of the decade, economic progress resumed a rapid pace. Transportation got a boost with the completion of a modern highway from Yuma to El Centro in 1925 and with the opening of the first scheduled commercial air service in 1926. The Mormon Temple, an imposing structure in Mesa, was completed in 1927, and Coolidge Dam, additional insurance against drought, was finished the next year. The stock market crash of 1929 was not felt immediately in Arizona, but the effects were not long in coming and there was little optimism as the decade drew to a close.

The Great Depression of the 1930s brought acute suffering to Arizona. Though the state was slow to feel the severest effects when compared with eastern states, it was also slow to recover. Arizona's population continued to grow throughout the Depression, although its rate of increase became less than at any other time in history. Even as early in the Depression as 1930, Arizona's population of 435,573 represented an increase of only 30 percent over the 1920 figure.

The following ten years showed a rate of growth of less

than half that percentage. Most mines closed and the few that operated worked on greatly reduced payrolls. Farm prices fell to almost nothing. Construction ceased and what little manufacturing there had been in the state disappeared. Very few people in the United States had enough money to go touring or vacationing to Arizona; therefore, many resorts and places of recreation closed or operated with a skeleton staff. Many of the immigrants to Arizona were refugees from other parts of the country, grateful for a warm winter climate if for nothing else. Thousands of unemployed boys were brought into the twenty-seven CCC camps established in Arizona. The conservation projects performed by these boys were of great benefit to Arizona, as many projects were accomplished that the State could not have afforded for many years. Mining and agriculture slowly began to crawl upward in 1936, but only mining made any real progress until World War II.

The population in 1940 was 499,261, an increase of only 15 percent over the 435,573 of 1930. The new spurt of growth in Arizona's business and population due to the war did not begin until 1942 when the prices of meat, copper, cotton and other commodities shot upward. Many military air bases and other training centers were established throughout the state, bringing thousands of servicemen and their families to Arizona. The relatively protected situation of Arizona, its year-round mild climate and the opportunity it afforded for industrial disbursement, brought industrial plants with government contracts into the state, establishing Arizona's potential for manufacturing. Many of the workers and owners of these plants were anxious to stay in Arizona after the war was over, and many servicemen who had been stationed here returned after release from the service. Though population losses occurred from 1943 to 1945, by 1946 more than 100,000 G.I.'s and their families had made Arizona their home. Many other postwar arrivals were people who had planned to retire in Arizona when the war was over.

They invested in land or industries, adding to Arizona's capital growth.

During World War II many major employers of the United States established operations in Arizona. Early during the wartime period the Navajo Ordinance Depot was established at Bellemont. Consolidated Vultee brought its operation to the Tucson area in 1943 and operated until cessation of hostilities in 1945. The aluminum plant in Maricopa County, just outside Phoenix at that time, was operated by Aluminum Company of America (Alcoa) from 1943 through 1946. AiResearch, a division of Garrett Corporation, operated a facility in Phoenix from 1942 through 1946. Also during the period, Goodyear Aircraft was very active in the Phoenix area. While many of these firms ceased operation at the end of hostilities, it is interesting to note that the same facilities were rapidly activated either during the period between World War II and the Korean Conflict or early during the rearmament period of the Korean outbreak.

During the postwar period the initial installation of Motorola was established in the Phoenix area. Also prior to 1950, Reynolds Aluminum Company reactivated the War Assets Administration plant near Phoenix that had been operated by Alcoa. This plant became one of the world's largest aluminum extrusion plants under one roof.

During the decade of the 1950s Arizona's population and economic growth, though war-inspired, had been proven to be not war-dependent. The population of the State reached 749,587 in 1950, an increase of more than 50 percent over that of 1940. This great increase of population was effective in causing tremendous growth in construction and trade, as well as increase in other branches of the economy. Manufacturing, although it had grown from practically nothing to an employment of almost 10 percent of the total, was only crawling compared to its future tremendous expansion during the 1950s. Changes in the tax laws and planned programs to bring manufacturing into the state were so successful early in the 1950s, that it became Arizona's major source of income by 1956. Cattle, cotton and vegetable prices remained good and income from tourism was excellent in this period.

The 1950s was the period of the greatest industrial expansion that Arizona had experienced since statehood. Perhaps in terms of percentage growth rates, the early territorial days outstripped the 1950s, but numerical growth incidental to the Korean outbreak and persistent growth since the end of the conflict have caused the 1950s to be called by many "Arizona's period of economic emergence."

Although World War II had seen many successful manufacturing establishments operated in this state, their existence was due primarily to military expediency. The advantages of excellent flying weather, location away from congested areas and available labor supply had far outweighed economic reasons that would have prevented location of manufacturing and processing industries. During the 1950s, however, Arizona was "discovered" by many major manufacturing establishments. AiResearch, which had a very successful history in Phoenix during World War II, reestablished a plant in the Phoenix area in 1951. Early in 1951, Hughes Aircraft chose Tucson as the site for its guided missile manufacturing establishments. Hughes also expanded rapidly and in recent years has maintained stable employment in the Pima County area. Infilco Corporation, a world-renowned manufacturer of water treatment and sewage treatment equipment, established their plant in Tucson in 1950.

Firms that were established and operated as a result of the Korean Conflict included the Grand Central Aircraft Company in Tucson, which operated from 1950 through 1954 modifying propeller and later jet powered aircraft. The same physical plant was selected late in 1954 as the site of an aircraft modification and test flight center by Douglas Aircraft. This firm operated in the Tucson area until the revised Military Expendi-

ture Program forced closure early in 1960. The Phoenix Parachute Company was established in 1951 and operated, with minor ups and downs in employment, through 1954. Other small
operations, many of which represented nationally known firms,
found sites for successful wartime production in the State of
Arizona.

In 1951 the Yuma Test Station was established as a proving ground for Army equipment. Many of the modern weapons
that found their way to the battlefields of Korea and Vietnam,
or that are now in our arsenal of defense, were first developed
and tested at this modern facility.

Fort Huachuca, as a frontier cavalry outpost, as a permanent infantry and cavalry station during World War I, as a division training post during World War II and as a training base for
ground troop aviation engineers for Korea, has had a profound
influence on the history of the Southwest since its establishment in 1877. In January of 1954, Army Headquarters announced that Fort Huachuca would be converted into the Army's
major electronic proving ground. With Fort Huachuca established as the major proving ground of Army equipment, Arizona became, in the eyes of many of the nation's major electronics equipment producers, an area well worthy of consideration for plant location. The growth of the electronics components industry in Arizona has been virtually unparalleled in any
other part of our nation. In 1955 Motorola Corporation announced the establishment of a second plant, followed by the
announcement in 1956 of the establishment of a third plant.
Also in 1956, the General Electric Corporation announced that
Phoenix had been selected as the site for its computer division.
In 1955 Sperry Rand Corporation announced that manufacturing establishments would be located in the Phoenix area. Other
smaller local plants also have grown tremendously in the electronic components manufacturing field during the period 1950
to 1960.

Aircraft and electronic equipment were not the only types of manufacturing employment growing in the state of Arizona during the decade of the fifties. Garment manufacturing plants found a healthy labor market and welcome reception, with particular emphasis on the period subsequent to 1952. Prior to 1952, only a few hundred persons found employment in the garment trades in this state, however near the end of 1960 almost 2,000 persons were so employed.

Naturally, with considerable population growth and gains in manufacturing, construction of highways, residences, commercial buildings, factories, and warehouses was at an all-time high during the period of the fifties. In 1956, however, perhaps one of the largest construction projects ever to be announced in the United States was awarded for an Arizona site when announcement was made of the Glen Canyon Dam Project. This project, located in upper Coconino County, involved the building of one of the nation's largest hydroelectric and water storage dams in a location very remote from population, labor force or construction materials. As a result, an entire new town—Page, Arizona—was established.

By 1960, Arizona's population was spurred onward by economic growth and had attained a level of 1,302,161. This represented an increase of 74 percent over the preceding ten years. The 1950's showed the most rapid percentage increase of any decade since the fabulous 1880s. It must be remembered that in the 1880's the railroads were completed to and through Arizona, allowing the ultimate development of the area. In one hundred years, Arizona had grown from a population of 6,482 to 1,302,161.

The Democratic Party dominated the politics of the new state until after the Second World War when newcomers saw in the Republican Party an alternative to the entrenched Democrats. In 1950, Howard Pyle became the third Republican governor since statehood. Barry Goldwater then led the maturing

Republicans to a 1952 senatorial victory, defeating Senate Majority Leader Ernest McFarland. Goldwater became a national figure for the conservative cause and eventually the presidential nominee for the Republican Party in 1964.

In elections Arizona has a closed primary, with crossover voting prohibited. Democrats vote for Democrats and Republicans vote for Republicans. In 1986, figures released by Secretary of State Rose Mofford showed that there were 702,274 Republicans, 669,741 Democrats and 176,741 Independents and others, for a total of 1,548,259. Tucson has a history of voting Democratic while Phoenix favors the Republican party.

Arizona has six congressional districts.
* 1st District, which includes parts of east Phoenix and the east Valley.
* 2nd District, which includes parts of south and west Phoenix, extends to Yuma, south of Nogales and takes in the western half of Tucson.
* 3rd District, which takes in parts of west and northwest Phoenix and extends to the northwestern corner of the state.
* 4th District, which includes parts of north and northeast Phoenix and extends to the northeastern corner of the state.
* 5th District, which takes in the eastern side of Tucson and extends to the southeastern corner of the state.
* 6th District, which covers northern and eastern portions of Maricopa County.

It is to be noted that Arizona has many military installations and retired military. These blocs of votes usually lean toward the Republican Party in Arizona. Sun City, the world-famous retirement center, usually favors Republican candidates in most elections.

Voter registration in Arizona bodes well for the GOP in

the future. A Republican governor was elected in 1998 and Maricopa County, the largest population county in the state, boosted its Republican registration almost two to one over the Democrats.

Chapter Six

STEAMBOATS ON THE COLORADO

No one liked the camels in Arizona. Assuredly they could carry much water and much heavier loads than a mule. They were much speedier, and were infinitely more two footed. Unfortunately they had one social problem that far outweighed all of their assets. Quite literally they stunk.
David Rees

Steamboats are seldom mentioned in stories of the early West. Yet for more than a half-century the Colorado River furnished the avenue of commerce for river towns, mines and, at times, for the railroads themselves.

The 1870s were the heyday of the river traffic with over one hundred men employed. Before 1890 the number had dwindled to less than 40 and the last boats stopped running around 1917. Their last stand seems to have been the short haul from Yuma to the mining town of Picacho.

In their day, however, the Colorado River steamers not only answered a distinct, economic need but wrote another colorful chapter in the West's history. Boilers and stamps for the mills at Prescott, La Paz and El Dorado were brought up river on fleet, vessels so built that they "could flat in a heavy dew"

51

and frequently had to, for the errant Colorado would leave a mud bank today right in the spot of yesterday's channel.

The first river steamers came in the holds of sailing ships from San Francisco, but soon Yankee ingenuity went to work and the bulk of the river fleet was built on the spot with only the boilers and engines imported. One of the world's most unique shipyards at Port Isabel, Mexico, served the river. It isn't on any map today but Port Isabel itself was a phenomenon. It was an American town built on the east bank of the river at the mouth—far down in Sonora, Mexico. Steamers were built, repaired and rebuilt at this unique town. Also unusual was the dry-dock at the shipyard, made by scooping out a trough in the silt. A steamer would be run in at high tide. There is a rise and fall of 22 feet, so at low tide the ship was high and dry. A mule team would take a scarper and build a dike back of the ship and there you had a dry dock.

When the steamer was ready for service again, the process was reversed. Other things at Port Isabel were different, too. The company warehouse was the hull of the old Cocopah, hauled up and its decks enclosed with shiplap.

In the 1860s the river boats were often run by rivals but in May 1877, the Southern Pacific reached the California side of the river and soon, thereafter, bought out the private steamer concerns. *The Pacific Tourist Guide* of 1879 announced:

"The steamers of the Colorado Steam Navigation Company leave Yuma weekly from January 1 to November 1, and during November and December, every alternate Saturday.

"Steamers leave for Camp Mojave every fifth week and continue to El Dorado Canyon from May 1 to November 1 if the weather permits. Yuma to Castle Dome; 35 miles with $5 fare; Ehrenburg, 125 miles; Aubrys, 220 miles, $28; Camp Mohave, 300 miles, $35; Hardville, 312 miles, $35; Dorado Canyon, 365 miles, $45."

It is reported that when the Yuma Indians saw the steamboat, they were terrified and ran crying that the devil was coming up the river blowing fire out his nose.

The early day pilots would have a hard time recognizing their river today. Civilization has harnessed the river of the West and, in so doing, has thrown six dams across it between Lake Mead and the international line. There are Laguna and the Imperial Dams, north of Yuma, where irrigation water is diverted for the Imperial Valley; Head Gate Rock Dam near Parker and Parker Dam, a few miles upstream; Davis Dam above Needles; and finally Hoover Dam.

The man-made lakes behind these barriers have buried landmarks, old town and the sites of the early day wharves. In other places the shifting channel has left old ports high and dry two or three miles from the present river.

Much of the colorful early history of Arizona is concerned with river navigation, which was a matter of skill and experience since there are constant difficulties and dangers to overcome. Sometimes at the mouth of the great stream tidal waves raged through the delta. Other problems in the lower river were shallows, concealed mud and sandbars; farther up the river were hidden pebble bars and submerged boulders. At times boats were grounded for days.

Upstream traffic carried general merchandise, mining and milling machinery, foods, and miscellaneous items, passengers, troops and military troop supplies. The downriver loads consisted of bullion, ores, hides, pelts, wood, passengers and troops. Each river town was a terminus of freight route; the principal points above Yuma were Ehrenberg for shipments to and from Wickenburg, and Hardyville for Prescott. Callville, the Mormon settlement on the Colorado a few miles below the Virgin River, was first reached by barge in 1866. It soon became an important shipping center for wagon transportation at Salt Lake City.

By 1850 activity around the junction of the Gila and

Colorado Rivers had increased to such an extent that Gen. Persifer Smith sent Lt. George H. Derby to make reconnaissance of the Colorado, from its mouth to Fort Yuma, with an idea of establishing a river route from the Gulf of California to the military reservation. If this could be accomplished, it would be possible to bring supplies from San Diego and San Francisco, much more cheaply than they could be brought by land over the desert route from the coast.

Derby and his party in the schooner, Invincible, under the command of Capt. Wilcox, arrived at the mouth of the Colorado in 1851. Because of the shallowness of the water, they would ascend the stream only about 24 miles. At this point the flatboats were used for another 60 miles. By then the expedition clearly showed the feasibility of the river route, and it was adopted immediately.

In the spring of 1851 another schooner, the Sierra Madre, under the command of George A. Johnson, arrived at the river's mouth with supplies for the troops at the fort. Shortly thereafter Ben Hartshorn, Capt. Wilcox and George Johnson made a contract with the federal government to bring stores from the schooners to Fort Yuma. The waters were so shallow about the mouth of the river that it was necessary to transfer all goods to barges and then tow the barges. This was the beginning of a profitable river trade on the Colorado.

Soon the Hartshorn, Wilcox, and Johnson company became the Colorado Steam Navigation Company. Although this new concern did not own a single boat when formed, it immediately purchased one that Capt. Turnbull had brought from San Francisco to the head of the Gulf. There the steamer was torn down, shipped to Robinson's Landing at Yuma, reassembled and named the Uncle Sam. She was sixty-five feet long, sixteen feet wide, and 3-1/2 feet deep. Like most river craft of those days, she was a side wheeler, powered by a locomotive boiler of twenty horsepower. After 3-1/2 years of service between the mouth of the river and Yuma, the Uncle Sam sank at her mooring at Pilot Knob, nine miles west of Yuma.

In 1854, Capt. Johnson, one of the navigation firm members, brought the steamer General Jessup to Yuma. This being her maiden voyage, she carried thirty-five tons of freight although her capacity was sixty tons in two feet of water. She was one hundred and four feet long, seventeen feet wide, and was powered by two fifty-horsepower engines. The General Jessup was the first steam-powered craft to ascend above Yuma when she carried mining supplies some twenty miles about Hardyville in 1858.

In 1854, the U.S. government paid 75 dollars a ton for transporting supplies from the mouth of the Colorado to Fort Yuma. The freight bill for 14 months amounted to $94,000.

Johnson later headed the exploration party of 1857 in the General Jessup. Of the latter trip he wrote:

> In December, 1857, I left Fort Yuma with the steamer General Jessup for the purpose of determining the navigability of the Colorado above Yuma. Captain William A. Winder was in charge. My crew consisted of an assistant pilot, fourteen or fifteen deck hands, and six mountain men and trappers. Our trip was attended by no particular difficulties.
>
> Late in December I arrived at a canyon in the Colorado which was not navigable. This was about seventy-five miles above Fort Mojave. At this point is the mouth of a canyon which comes in from the west known as El Dorado. Knowing I had reached the height of practical navigation, I turned back.
>
> The next day I landed on the east bank for wood. While lying there an expedition came in

sight which proved to be that of Gen. E.F. Beale.

While making a trip to the mining camp of Picacho, the General Jessup struck a submerged boulder and sank. Fortunately, the Colorado Navigation Company had another seaworthy ship called the Colorado Number One. This vessel was dispatched to the assistance of the ill-fated General Jessup. Eventually, the sunken craft was raised and towed to Yuma for repairs. Some months later she returned to service. The unlucky schooner finally came to an end when one of her boilers exploded while she was running the rapids near Ogden's Landing, about twenty-five miles above Lerdo Colony, which is a few miles above the mouth of the river. Two men were killed in the explosion and the boat was condemned. Her machinery was removed and shipped to San Francisco; her hull was towed to Menturn Slough and sunk.

The Colorado Number Two was constructed at the Yuma shipyards during the Civil War, the fifth vessel to be put in service by The Colorado Steam Navigation Co. The shipyard at Port Isabel was the more popular place for repairing and building vessels, but great caution was taken in erecting the Colorado Number Two, because of the fear that a Confederate cruiser might invade the waters around Port Isabel and destroy the ship before it was completed.

The Colorado Number Two, like her predecessor the Colorado Number One, was put into service on the river and navigated between the river's mouth and points as far north as Fort Mojave, which was over two hundred miles north of Yuma. In March 1878, she was taken into the shipyards and given a complete overhaul. This was done by taking out every defective plank from her bottom and replacing them with new ones. Her seams were recaulked and pitched, and her bottom painted with coal tar. Also due to the presence of a great deal of driftwood on the water's surface, the ship's bottom was fitted out with large knobs under her counters for future protection against the menace.

After faithfully serving her owner for over fifteen years, the Colorado Number Two went to the bottom of the muddy stream. Her haul was moved out at Port Isabel and used as a foundation for a large warehouse, which later burned and nearly destroyed the entire port. Her machinery, being still in good condition, was dismantled and shipped to San Francisco, where it was later used on the Hattie Picket, a steamer plying the Sacramento River.

A competitive boat line came into existence on the Colorado River when the surrounding regions experienced a mining boom about 1858. This new company was founded by Capt. T.E. Trueworthy, owner of the steamer, Esmeraldo, which had been navigated from San Francisco to Port Isabel under the command of Capt. C. C. Overman. Capt. Trueworthy had been operating a steamship business on the Sacramento River before coming to the Colorado region in 1861. In this year he purchased the steamer, Nina Tilden, in San Francisco and organized the Pacific Colorado Navigation Company.

The new competing steamboat line lasted only about six years. The end came in 1867 when the Colorado Steam Navigation Company purchased the steamers Esmeraldo and Nina Tilden, and the barges Black Crook and White Fawn.

After selling out the Colorado Steam Navigation Company, Capt. Trueworthy invested a small fortune in another sailing venture. He converted a large 182-foot Sacramento River barge into a four-masted schooner, and christened the craft the Victoria. The intention of the owner was to load her with lumber, send her to China and construct barges for use on the Yangtze River. But instead of going to the Orient, the Victoria, under the command of C.E. Qualin, left San Francisco for the mouth of the Colorado River with 4,000,000 feet of lumber, fifty tons of groceries and 800 barrels of whiskey. Her voyage from the seacoast port was uneventful and she anchored twenty-five miles up the river. While riding at anchor, a strong, incoming tide caused her to drift over her own anchor, and a protruding fluke tore a hole in her bottom. The ship stayed afloat, probably because she carried 4,000,000 feet of lumber. Later she was towed to Starvation Point, about 125 miles south of Yuma, and tied near the bank. There the Indians, for some unknown reason, set fire to the weeds and underbrush. The flames, rapidly spreading, finally reached the Victoria. The groceries were saved, the lumber was set free and floated out to sea, but the whiskey is reported to still be resting on the bottom of the river. This catastrophe nearly ruined Captain Trueworthy financially.

The Colorado Navigation Company was very prosperous from the day it started business. At one time there were 12 steamers and as many barges operating on the river between its mouth and Yuma and points north of Yuma. She was 128 feet long and 28 feet wide, and was constructed at the river's mouth in 28 days by Charley Overman, Charley Tyson, and Jack Mellon. The White Fawn was built in 1864, and lengthened in 1867. She was constructed in San Francisco, and sent in pieces and assembled at Port Isabel.

In 1867 the barge, Pumpkin Seed, loaded with iron, was moored to Jaeger's Landing in Yuma, when a heavy rain came and filled her, causing her to sink.

During all these early years when the steamboat company was operating, the offices occupied four rooms in an old adobe building along the river's edge in Yuma. It was in this building that the various boat captains and construction experts were called together to plan new river crafts as fast as the trade demanded them.

The people of the Yuma area had sent numerous petitions to Congress asking aid in making the river safer for navigation; and in 1870 a sum of money was appropriated to purchase a steam barge for dredging. This craft was brought to

Yuma, where it caused much commotion because of the rumor that it was a Mexican gunboat, flying the American flag. The barge was used for several years in dredging above Needles, California, and greatly helped navigation on the river. It was later sold to an individual by the name of Whitcombe, who used it for a pleasure barge.

Navigation on the Colorado River was not all pleasure, but it was not all grief. When the weather was cool, many of the trips were very enjoyable and scenic. It is recorded that the steamer, Cocopa, made a round trip from Hardyville to Camp El Dorado, a distance of about one hundred and twenty miles, in a little less than twenty-four hours.

In 1874, a distance of two hundred miles consumed eleven days by stage coach. The pleasure trip experienced by Hardy was far different from what Mrs. Martha Summerhayes endured while going from Fort Yuma to Mojave.

Mrs. Summerhayes and her husband, a lieutenant in the army, sailed up the river on the Gila which was loaded with supplies and towed a barge full of soldiers. The thermometer varied from 107°F to 122°F in the shade. Even at night it was impossible to sleep in the staterooms. Mrs. Summerhayes described the situation as follows:

> And thus began another day of intolerable glare and heat . . . There was nothing to relieve the monotony of the scenery. On each side of us, low river banks, and nothing between those and the horizon line. . . at last on the 8th of September, we arrived at Fort Mohave, 11 days from Fort Yuma. "A quick trip," said the Captain. I listened and wondered if I had heard right, for those 11 days in midsummer on the Great Colorado had burned themselves into my memory.

59

In 1858 Lt. Joseph C. Ives was steaming up the Colorado River in an iron boat called the Explorer, for the purpose of determining whether or not the stream was navigable. With much pushing and towing, the clumsy craft finally reached Black Canyon and then almost met with disaster near the spot where Hoover Dam is located. Following the exploratory trip, the boat was sold and then disappeared from the pages of history. Within recent years the craft has been rediscovered, almost buried in the silt of the Colorado River delta—and its skeleton is still to be seen there. Here is one part of the story about one of the most thrilling episodes in the history of the Southwest:

> We were shooting past the entrance to Black Canyon," wrote Lt. Joseph C. Ives in his mariner's log book on March 8, 1858, "when the Explorer with a stunning crash, brought up abruptly and instantaneously against a sunken rock. For a second the impression was that the canyon had fallen in. The concussion was so violent that the men near the bow were thrown overboard; the doctor, Mr. Mollhausen and myself, having been seated in front of the upper deck, were precipitated head foremost into the bottom of the boat; the fireman who was pitching a log into the fire, went halfway in with it; the boiler was thrown out of place; the steam pipe doubled up; the wheelhouse was torn away, and it was expected the boat would fill in and sink instantly by all.

Thus ended, after three and one-half months of arduous labor, the initial cruise of the Explorer, the iron steamboat commissioned by the U.S. War Department. in 1857, to determine whether or not the Colorado River was a navigable stream.

The Explorer was built in Philadelphia. It was a 56-foot

sternwheel steamer. After a brief trial run on the Delaware River, it was knocked down in eight sections, shipped by boat overland to the Pacific, again by boat to San Francisco, and finally to the mud flats at the head of the Gulf of California, to be assembled for the trip up the river as far as it would go.

It was built of iron, with a huge boiler mounted in the center of the deck. The boiler was too heavy. To correct this weakness and give the craft longitudinal stability, four long wooden beams were bolted to the bottom. Needless to say, this clumsy makeshift creature caused no end of trouble in navigating the countless bars in the channel of the lower Colorado.

Accompanying Lt. Ives on the expedition were A.J. Carrol of Philadelphia as engineer; Dr. J.S. Newberry, physician and geologist; F.W. Egoffstein, who had been a member of the Fremont expedition in 1853, topographer; P.H. Taylor and meteorological assistant, H.B. Mollhausen, artist and collector in natural history. Lt. Tipton, 3rd artillery, and 25 soldiers from the garrison at Yuma served as military escort. Due to the limited capacity of the boat, the soldiers traveled overland with pack-train. It was an escort in name only, since the troops left Yuma several days after the Explorer steamed away, and did not catch up with the river expedition until Ives reached Mojave Valley on his return trip.

Lt. Ives completed the reconnaissance without serious mishap and, on the basis of his report to Secretary of War John F. Floyd in 1869, the Colorado was declared to be a navigable stream.

A few months after the return of the expedition the Explorer was sold by the government to Yuma rivermen who planned to use it for freighting on the Colorado. According to old Arizona records quoted by Godfrey Sykes in his book, *The Colorado Delta*, after a few trips hauling wood, the steamer broke away from its moorings near Pilot Knob, floated downstream and disappeared from sight. Thus ended the first chapter in the saga of the good ship Explorer. Seventy years passed. The men who had piloted the Explorer and stoked mesquite wood in its huge boiler remained as living names only to those students of history who had read the fine records left by Lt. Ives.

Then, in 1929, word came out of the mesquite and willow jungle that covers the delta of the Colorado. An aged Indian named Clabasa had seen the rusted hulk of an old barge partly buried in the silt of a channel long abandoned by the fickle waters of the Colorado.

The story of the white man's rediscovery of this boat was told by Gus Seligman, member of an engineering party engaged in surveying the Colorado Delta. Seligman covered nearly every foot of the vast silt plain by car, horseback or on foot. He said:

> Tony, my brother, Dirk, and I later found the remains of the boat, early in 1929. We took pictures of it and began to look up its history. About six months later, C.N. Perry joined us in our work, identified the crafts as Ives' Explorer, and wrote an article about it for the American Society of Civil Engineers. At the time we found the boat there wasn't much left. It reminded me of a carcass after the coyotes and buzzards were through with it. Only the bones remained.

By 1878 when the railroad bridged the Colorado at Yuma, the steamers Mohave and Gila were the oldest boats in operation. These had been in service for 20 years. In order to prevent any competition, the Southern Pacific Railroad bought out the Colorado Steam Navigation Company in the same year it bridged the river.

The river trade decreased considerably after the coming

of the railroad, but several steamers were built either at the Yuma shipyards or at Port Isabel, Mexico, during the eighties. These were known as the Searchlight, Cochan and St. Valier. The Searchlight happened to be above Laguna Dam when it was completed in 1900, and had to be lifted over the structure by the government.

The other great river in Arizona is the Gila. Many years before Columbus came to the Americas, thousands of people lived along the Gila. In particular, three cultures dominated the Gila area: the Anasazi, the Hohokam and the Mogollon. Their greatest achievement was the invention of the atlatl, or spear thrower.

The Gila has its beginnings in the Mogollon Mountains and runs the width of the state. It flows into the Colorado River at the famed Yuma Crossing. It is about 600 miles long and was the center of much of the history in this state. Many people followed its path on the way to California. It had many names such as: Totonteac, River of the name of Jesus, Blue, Blaufuss, Poison, Helay, River of the Sun and River of the Apostles. As an institution, it was the bread and butter of Arizona.

It is to be noted that people have been living along the Gila for about 25,000 years. Hence, people were living there before they were living in any of the other 49 states. Numerous ball courts were excavated along the Gila showing that the early settlers played some kind of a game like soccer. A rubber ball was found by archaeologists and it is now in the Southwest Museum in Los Angeles. Research has found about 50 ball courts along the Gila which tells us that the people had a high degree of civilization. Games seem to indicate a higher degree of culture and leisure than the nomad cultures of other peoples.

Chapter Seven

MINING

There are two poisonous spiders in Arizona. They are the black widow and the brown recluse. They both enjoy locating in such fly-infested places as outdoor privies. People using these toilets, unaware that they are invading the sanctuary of these normally shy spiders, have been bitten in the most sensitive and unmentionable places.

Marshall Trimble
in his book, *Arizona*

The history of Arizona is inextricably tied to mining. From the earliest days, silver mines had been worked by the Spanish whenever there were sufficient troops to provide protection against the Apaches. The Mowry and Heintzelman Silver Mines near Patagonia and Tubac in Santa Cruz County were being worked in the late 1850s. The rich gold placer deposits along the Gila and Colorado Rivers were discovered in 1858, and the gold placers on the Hassayampa and Lynx Creeks were located in 1863. Henry Wickenburg discovered the Vulture Mine in 1863. This mine was the most productive of Arizona's early gold mines. The Peoples Party made a rich find at Antelope Hill near present-day Yarnell; and a little later all of these rich strikes not only brought in a tremendous influx of miners, but also helped to build a solid foundation for Arizona commerce and demonstrated the territory's value to the Union. To keep these riches for the U.S. Treasury, Congress was impelled to grant Arizona separate territorial status in 1863 and detail sufficient troops to hold it against the Confederacy.

The prospectors, who joined the great rush to Arizona after the Civil War, did such a thorough job that most of Arizona's primary mineral discoveries were made from 1865 to 1880. These included not only the Silver King and Silver Queen Mines, but also all the richest copper deposits including those at Clifton-Morenci, Globe, Ray, Bisbee and Jerome. Prior to 1870, however, copper was not important as the demand was not sufficient to pay for complicated processing and high transportation costs. Silver on top and copper below is a common occurrence in Arizona so that many present-day copper mines originally were worked only for silver.

The passage of the Sherman Silver Purchase Act in 1890 demonetizing silver, along with the fact that the richest and most easily obtainable ore in the mines was nearly exhausted, brought an end to silver mining by 1900, except as a by-product. Gold mining, however, continued to be a significant factor in Arizona's economy until after World War I. The postwar depression in 1921 drastically reduced gold mining activities until 1932, when there was a small upswing which lasted until the gold mine closing order in 1942. Since then Arizona's gold production has consisted only of that produced as a by-product of the mining of other metals.

The earliest copper mine to produce in Arizona was at Ajo. It had such extremely rich ore that a small profit would be made in spite of the tremendous costs of shipping the ore by mule train to the Gulf, where it was loaded on ships and sent to the nearest smelter in Swansea, Wales. The Ajo Mine was worked on this basis from 1855 to 1861, after which the ore was no longer rich enough to make this method of mining profitable.

By the 1870s, industrialists, capitalists and miners were beginning to sense the potential importance of copper. All the fairly rich deposits were developed in this period and smelters were built to handle the bonanza copper ores of the time. In 1886 the first concentrator which made lower grade, porphyry ores profitable was built at Morenci. From that time on, as richness of the ore declined, the copper industry compensated by inventing new methods for profitable mining.

In 1908 Arizona became the nation's top producer of copper. It lost first place in 1909 to Montana but regained it in 1910 and has held it ever since.

The postwar depression closed most of Arizona's mines in 1921; but they recovered rapidly, reopened in 1922 and did well until the depression following the stock market crash of 1929. By 1932 all of the mines had either reduced operations to bare minimum essential for maintenance or had closed entirely. Not one of the state's major mining corporations failed during this period. Beginning in 1935 most of the mines reopened and production was gradually increased by the mining of low-grade ores through open-pit operation. In 1939 signs of impending conflict in Europe became unmistakable and Arizona's legislature, recognizing the great demands that war would make on Arizona's mining industry, created the Arizona Department of Mineral Resources to aid the industry in every way possible. After December 7, 1941, the United States acted to spur copper production by offering loans and premium prices to developers of marginal ore deposits and over-quota premiums to owners of established mines which increased their production. These incentives, together with the reduction of available manpower and man-hour production, accelerated efforts to devise ways and means by which machine power could be utilized to produce copper.

New drilling and blasting techniques, full-revolving electric shovels and diesel locomotives are a few examples of the numerous innovations which were introduced to improve production and efficiency of mining operations. Federal government assistance made possible the exploration of low-grade deposits and the very expensive preparation of properties for the use of block-caving mining methods. The development of simplified mill machinery enabled mill operators to use women workers, partially to relieve the manpower shortage.

Contrary to pessimistic predictions, the end of World War II in 1945 did not bring a reduction in the need for copper and other Arizona metals. The pent-up domestic demand for products unavailable during the war, coupled with "Cold War" arms race and the Korean Conflict in 1950, actually called for an increase in metal production.

The mining industry continues to play a vital part in Arizona's economy.

Copper annually accounts for approximately 85 percent of all minerals produced in Arizona. Moreover, the output of most other metals largely is a by-product of copper mining. Sand and gravel are the largest nonmetallic minerals produced locally.

Arizona is rich in coal. Geologists claim the state has enough coal deposits for its energy needs to last for one hundred years.

Arizona is also blessed with tremendous salt deposits around Glendale, Phoenix, Kingman, Eloy and Tucson. Of all the deposits, only the West Glendale area is currently being mined. Nearly 1 million tons of salt have been excavated there in the past 15 years.

MINERALS BY COUNTY

County	Principal Minerals Produced in Each County
Apache	Petroleum, helium, clays, pumice, sand and gravel, natural gas, stone.
Cochise	Copper, stone, lime, sand and gravel, gold, silver.
Coconino	Pumice, sand and gravel, stone.
Gila	Copper, lime, stone, asbestos, sand and gravel, silver, gold, molybdenum, clays.
Graham	Sand and gravel, copper, pumice.
Greenlee	Copper, lime, silver, gold, stone, sand and gravel.
Maricopa	Sand and gravel, lime, stone, clays, mica, salt.
Mohave	Copper, molybdenum, sand and gravel, silver, feldspar, gold, stone.
Navajo	Coal, sand and gravel, iron ore, pumice, stone.

Pima

Copper, molybdenum, cement, silver, sand and gravel,stone, gold, lime, lead, clays, zinc, mica.

Pinal

Copper, molybdenum, gold, silver, sand and gravel, lime, gypsum, stone, perlite, pyrites, clays.

Santa Cruz

Zinc, sand and gravel, lead, stone.

Yavapai

Copper, cement, zinc, sand and gravel, molybdenum, stone, lime silver, gypsum, lead, clays, golds, pumice.

Yuma

Sand and gravel, stone, lead, silver, gold, zinc, tungsten.

Chapter Eight

THE PERALTA TREASURE
IN THE SUPERSTITION MOUNTAINS

Every history student knows about the tale of the Dutchman and his gold mine in the Superstition Mountains located in Apache Junction, Arizona. But few know and very few history books narrate the story of the Peralta family and the role they played in those mountains and how they were tied to rich treasure.

It all began with a shipwreck of a Spanish ship off the coast of Florida around the year 1528. There were a few Spanish survivors of that shipwreck headed by a Spaniard by the name of Cabeza de Vaca and his slave, a black man by the name of Estevan.

This small group of Spaniards were to penetrate the American Southwest after being captured by the Indians. The Indians did not kill them for they pawned themselves off as medicine men. After some time they learned the Indian language, customs and eating habits. The Indians also showed them their gold and silver and told them about the fabulous seven cities of gold located in the north of New Spain.

Later in time it was Marcos de Niza, a Spanish padre,

along with Estevan, who went on an exploratory mission look-ing for the seven cities of gold, only to come back with no suc-cess. Eventually Mendoza, the viceroy in Mexico City, inter-viewed Cabeza de Vaca who, in turn, told him all he had learned in talking with many Indian tribes about the seven cities of gold. The viceroy by now was so excited about what he had heard, that, in 1540, he decided to act by organizing a huge army of some 300 soldiers and hundreds of Indians and guides to march from Mexico City in search of the seven cities. This group was to be known as the Coronado expedition. It was financed from the personal monies of both Mendoza and Coronado.

Coronado was named captain general of the biggest ar-mada ever assembled at that time in the New World with one purpose, and that was to find the New World to see God, glory and gold. It was quite evident to all that gold took first place.

Coronado discovered no gold, no silver and no glory. In 1542 he led his tattered army back to Culican, Mexico. Fewer than a hundred of the faithful were with him when he arrived in Mexico City to report to Viceroy Mendoza. For later genera-tions his journey was no failure for he gave us invaluable infor-mation about the Southwest and a vivid description of the Indi-ans. He gave up two years of his young life. The journey was stressful on his health and he died at the age of 44. He had gone all the way from Mexico City to Benson, Arizona, and all the way east to Wichita, Kansas. Today the Coronado National Monument and the Coronado National Forest honor his name.

Coronado was followed by the Mexican explorer, Espejo, who was excited when he learned about the stories of riches being circulated by the Indians. In the vicinity of Jerome, Ari-zona, Espejo discovered mines of great value. He then hurried to Mexico with his ore specimens.

Another explorer who came on the scene was Governor Juan de Ornate of New Mexico, who established a colony in New Mexico in 1598. His wife was the granddaughter of Cortes.

One of his followers, being financed by the governor, discovered some rich mines near Prescott, Arizona. Governor Onate was banished from the territory of New Mexico for being very cruel to the Indians, concealing riches for his personal use and other offenses. But in the final analysis, Espejo, Coronado and Onate succeeded only in making the area of the Southwest better known to Europeans.

From that time nothing of any great consequence happened in the area of the Southwest until the coming of the Peraltas. They were a Spanish family of great note who are not well known in American history books but who are the source of many legends centering in their vast mining treasures which were buried in the Superstition Mountains in Arizona. And, they are the focal point of this manifesto. Many tales of storytellers surround the history of this remarkable family.

History records that one of the Peraltas was governor of Cadiz, Spain, in the early seventeenth century while a Pedro Peralta was governor of New Mexico in 1609 and became the founder of Santa Fe, New Mexico. The family coming from Spain seemed to have made Arizpe, Mexico their original home.

Many in the family also served in the Spanish military and held high rank; many in the family also received sundry land grants for outstanding service to the kings of Spain. It was these land grants that made the Peraltas famous in the history of Spain and in America. However, much of the history is hidden in countless legends and storytelling. It is hard for the historian to distinguish between true history and fiction.

History records many land grants that were given by the Spanish rulers to favorites who helped and aided the Spanish empire. In Arizona alone there were seventeen land grants recorded and California had even more. The University of California at Berkeley lies on a Peralta land grant. The land grant that caused the greatest consternation is the alleged one given by King Ferdinand VI of Spain in 1748 to the Peralta family.

The Peralta land grant was recorded for all to see in the public records in Guadalajara, Mexico, in 1768. On January 22, 1776, the official confirmation was given by King Carlos III of Spain and it was mapped by Padre Phefferkorn, a well known Jesuit author at that time.

The huge Peralta grant was not an ordinary land claim. A rectangle stretching from the present day Sun City, Arizona in the northeast corner to Silver City, New Mexico, it covered 11 million acres and included Phoenix, Mesa, Tempe, Globe, Clifton, the Superstition Mountains, Apache Junction, parts of the Southern Pacific Railroad and the rich Silver King mine. Not too far south were the wealthy mines of Tombstone, Arizona. All in all it was a premature Fort Knox in riches. Even the famed Father Kino, the Jesuit who founded some 13 missions in the Arizona Territory, reported in his diary that he saw rich mines in his travels.

The Peralta family took quick advantage of the gold and silver in the area of the Superstition Mountains and had about 18 mines in those mountains. The Spanish and Mexicans dominated the area. The King of Spain was to obtain 20 percent of the loot but Madrid was too far away, so the Peraltas enriched their own holdings and shared it with the Roman Catholic Church, according to the storytellers and legends that have been passed down through the ages. We have little accurate history of those times. We do know that in 1848, when the Americans were intent on taking over the whole of the Southwest, the Peraltas were in a severe crisis.

According to the Treaty of Guadalupe Hidalgo signed in 1848, the Americans now were in control of the whole Southwest. It was imperative that the Peraltas had to take their holdings and move to Mexico. They made a stop in the Superstition Mountains probably to pick up more gold which they had stored from their many mines. While there, they noticed large numbers of Apaches and other Indian tribes who had been following them. The Spanish had been very cruel to the Indians; there was no love lost between them. This was a time for revenge and the Indians wanted it before the Peraltas reached Mexico. About 3,000 Indians, so the legend says, had been gathered for this last roundup. They attacked over a period of days and all of the Peralta party were killed. It was one of the famous massacres in American history, however, most American history students know nothing about it. To this day there is a special area in the Superstitions that is called the "Peralta Massacre Grounds". It must be noted that the Peraltas knew that once they were in the Superstitions it was unlikely they would escape. So they quietly hid all their gold and rich possessions in seven special sites. This was done before the massacre. To this day no one has found them. Over the years hundreds of miners have tried to unravel the mystery as to where this treasure is. Legend has it that Jacob Waltz, who roamed the mountains surrounding the Salt River Valley for two decades searching for gold, found one of the mines when he struck gold in those mountains. The old Dutchman died in 1891 but his legends still live.

Today the Superstition Mountains are the reservoirs of three major hidden treasures:

1. The Dutchman's gold mine.

2. The Peralta Treasure.

3. The Jesuit Treasures.

None have ever been found to this day.

The Jesuit Fathers are Roman Catholic priests who belong to an order founded by Ignatious Loyola in 1534 in Madrid, Spain, where the headquarters of the society resides to this day. The group is officially known as the Society of Jesus or in short, thc Jesuits. Loyola wanted them to be like soldiers fighting for the causes of the Roman Catholic Church. Hence, he wanted them very well educated and they had to weather a seminary training of about 20 years from from high school before they could be ordained into the Catholic priesthood. Their focus was to be in education and in missionary work. For this reason, they were very active in the New World and wherever the Spanish conquistadores went, they followed. History continually accounts for their presence by calling them the "Black Robes". They give complete obedience to the Pope. The most famous Jesuit was Father Kino.

In 1767 the King of Spain expelled the Jesuits from all parts of the New World. In many areas they were indirectly involved with mining. Their vast network of missions and good works called for financial aid of great proportions. While the King of Spain was to receive 20 percent of all the gold, much of it went to the Jesuits. So when the Jesuits left, where did their share of the gold go? Some of it was hidden in the Superstition Mountains, according to legend and the often repeated stories of professional storytellers. The Jesuits wcre expelled for many reasons from Spanish America but one of the main reasons was their lack of cooperation in seeing that the Spanish king received his twenty percent. Also there was constant friction between the focus of the royalty and their rules versus the goals and regulations of Christian principles of the Jesuits. There is no doubt that the Jesuits controlled much of the great wealth of the New World but it was a hidden wealth and very difficult to prove historically. It is felt that in the final analysis the Jesuits could do more good for all than the sometimes wicked courts of the royalty. So if the Jesuits took some gold, who would throw the first stone?

It must be noted here that the Indians were not interested in gold. They never went out of their way to set up their own mines, rather the Spaniards used them as slaves in the mines.

So the mines belonged to the white man. To have gold in their hands would bring bad luck to the Indians.

Not too much happened of any consequence in the past quarter century in the Superstition Mountains until five Americans came upon the scene, Americans who are deeply interested in the educational impact of the mountains. They want to make sure that Americans today and American students of tomorrow will understand more fully that these mountains are incredible sources of great American history. Our American history books do not give them the importance they deserve. They have Titanic data that all American should know, and therefore, could be the most important mountains in America. The five Americans are: Ron Eagle, Robert Miller, Wags Wagner, Tony Diamond, Ph.D. and Robert Woznicki, Ph.D.

Chapter Nine

ARIZONA'S FIFTEEN COUNTIES

We rode the big cavalry horses over the sands of the Maricopa desert, swung in our hammocks under the ramadas; swam in the red waters of the Verde River, ate canned peaches, pink butter and commissary hams, listened for the scratching of the centipedes as they scampered around the edges of our canvas-covered floor, found scorpions in our slippers, and rattlesnakes under our beds.

Martha Summerhays
wife of an Army officer
Camp McDowell, Arizona, 1865

Arizona has 15 counties. This chapter contains a short history of each one. The history of the State of Arizona is very much a part of the history of these counties. Unlike counties in many other states, each county in Arizona is so rich with its folklore and culture that each could be a history book in itself. Only three of the counties have non-Indian names.

APACHE COUNTY: Apache County was created out of the eastern two-fifths of Yavapai County on February 24, 1879.

Before this division Yavapai County included, roughly, the northern half of that part of the state which lies east of Yuma and Mohave Counties. In 1881 part of the southern Apache county between the Black and Gila Rivers was cut off to form part of Graham County and later, in 1895, the remainder of Apache County was nearly halved, and the western portion became Navajo County. Apache County's present area is 7,151,360 acres. Snowflake was designated the county seat when it was first formed. After the first elections in the fall of 1879, the county government was set up at St. Johns, which in 1880 St. Johns was superseded by Springerville. Springerville remained the county seat for only two years until 1882, when St. Johns again became the county seat and has remained so to the present time.

Apache County was named for the Indians of Arizona and New Mexico. The Apaches did not exist as a single group or nation, but the term had been adopted as applying comprehensively to many tribes known for their warlike characteristics. Even the Navajos were considered Apaches as late as 1800.

Cattle raising and farming were the main sources of livelihood for the earliest settlers in what is now Apache County. In the early 1900's lumbering operations were begun in the White Mountains. Though many family farms are still operating in Apache County, most of the economic activity in that part of the county that is not set aside for the Navajo Reservation is based on tourism, livestock and forest products. The reservation area of the county depends heavily on federal Bureau of Indian Affairs activities, sheep raising and logging. Tourism to Canyon de Chelly promises to become more important as roads are improved. Oil and gas exploration in the Four Corners area and the helium extraction plant in the Pinta Dome site have improved the economic outlook for Apache County. The earliest known non-Indian settlement in Apache County was the Mexican community of Concho, established in the late 1860's and still in existence. The community was taken over in 1879 by Mormon settlers who called the town Erastus for a short time, but returned to the name Concho in 1890.

The next known settlement, which is still an active community today, is Springerville. In 1875 Harry Springer established a store, bringing merchandise from Albuquerque. The place was known as Springer's Store. Springer made the mistake of trusting outlaws with feed and seed and soon went broke. The townspeople jokingly called their town Springerville after he left, and that was the name given to the post office when it was established in 1879.

Shortly after Springer's failure and departure, Julius and Gustav Becker established a store in the same area in August of 1876. The Beckers used ox trains to bring in supplies until 1890, when they changed to horses and mules. After 1895 a branch railroad was completed to Magdalena, New Mexico, to speed transportation. The Becker Store is still the main store in Springerville. A son of Gustav Becker helped to establish the first transcontinental highway. The first automobile to make the coast-to-coast trip was driven through Springerville in 1910. Springerville today attracts many summer visitors due to its cool climate, recreational facilities, and good hunting and fishing.

St. Johns, at the site of an early Little Colorado River crossing, was first called El Vadito by Spanish explorers. In 1873 Solomon Barth, an Indian trader, won cattle and land in a poker game played with Mexicans who had settled at the crossing. He remained there with his brother Nathan and Morris, changing the name from El Vadito to San Juan (Spanish for St. John). Other white men had established cattle ranches near San Juan and the name was Americanized to St. Johns some time before 1879, when it first became the county seat. In 1875 Solomon Barth sold his interests to a Mormon agent, but the Mormons did not start a community there until 1880. This community was called Salem and was a mile north of St. Johns. It was abandoned about six months later when the Mormons moved into St. Johns. This move assured the continuation of the settlement.

Another early town in Apache County which is still active today is Eager, established in 1888 on ground given to the town by John, Joel and William Eager, who had homesteaded in Round Valley in 1878. Eagar was the site of an outlaw battle in which nine members of the Snider Gang were killed. The exact date of the fracas is in doubt, but it probably took place prior to 1900.

McNary was originally called Cluff Cienega after a Mormon bishop named Cluff. It gradually grew into a sawmill town as the lumbering industry developed in the White Mountains during the early 1900's. The lumber company called the town Coolley in honor of Corydon E. Cooley, a famous Indian scout under General Crook. When the McNary Lumber Company bought the property in 1924, the name was changed to McNary.

Principal industries: lumbering, tourism, livestock, forest products.

Points of interest: Petrified National Forest, Painted Desert, Canyon de Chelly, Monument Valley, Four Corners, Window Rock, Navajo Tribal Headquarters.

Recreation areas: Big and Crescent Lakes, Apache Reservation, Sunrise Ski Lodge, McNary and Eager Wood Products, Concho Country Club.

County Seat: St. Johns.

Elevation: 5,650 feet.

COCHISE COUNTY: Cochise County, named for Cochise, the famous leader of the Chiricahua Apache Indians, came into existence on February 1, 1881. Its area was originally the southeastern corner of Pima County. Tombstone was the first county seat and remained so until 1929 when the county offices were moved to Bisbee, which had become far more active and pros-perous. The present area of the county is 4,003,840 acres—as large an area as the states of Connecticut and Rhode Island to-gether.

The first census figure pertaining to what is now Cochise County was for Apache Pass in 1870. This was a very strategic settlement as it was on the only trail through the Chiricahua Mountains, the main Apache stronghold in Arizona. The Butterfield Overland Stage established a station at Apache Pass in 1857 to provide protection for its passengers. The pass formed a perfect ambush spot, and Apaches slaughtered passengers of stagecoaches and whole wagon trains without danger to them-selves. Early in 1858 President Butterfield asked the federal government to establish a fort, but he suspended operations in southern Arizona before Fort Bowie was established in 1862. The official post office name was not changed from Apache Pass to Fort Bowie until 1880. The fort has since been aban-doned, and the land was sold at public auction in 1911.

Gold and silver at Tombstone and copper at Bisbee were discovered in the same year—1877—but copper ore was so much more difficult to process that most of the early develop-ment occurred at Tombstone. The present Willcox area was the next to be developed when the coming of the railroad provided an opportunity to establish a shipping center for cattle. The eco-nomic history of Cochise County has been closely tied to the fortunes of the copper mining industry and the military estab-lishment at Fort Huachuca. In recent years agriculture has be-come economically important, with many diversified crops be-ing grown; and cattle raising has become continually impor-tant. The future looks bright for the county with recent expan-sion of the Lavender Pit Mine, the construction and operation of the Electronic Environmental Test Corridor and industrial growth in Douglas and Willcox.

Tombstone first appeared in the Census of 1880 with a

population of 973. The fame of the rich silver and gold discoveries drew thousands of people, including a goodly number of outlaws. Between 1880 and 1890 the town grew to a reputed 15,000 population— larger than San Francisco— and was considered the most cultured city in the entire Southwest. Well-known musicians and actors of the world played at the Bird Cage Theatre during these few years. In 1888 the mines began flooding and the town withered rapidly. Its population had dropped to less than two thousand by 1890, and it was virtually a ghost town until recent years. Tombstone is now a world-renowned attraction for tourists who come to see the locale of famous outlaw battles, Boothill Cemetery and the Bird Cage Theatre Museum. It is also home to many who work at Fort Huachuca. Recent oil exploration shows promise and might possibly bring another boom to Tombstone.

Bisbee was founded on the mining of copper rather than the more precious metals and, due to the more difficult extraction processes, did not attract the sudden rush of get-rich-quick people as did Tombstone. However, when Bisbee did start to grow as capital for mine development became available, its economic base proved to be more stable than Tombstone's. Original financial backing came from Judge Bisbee of San Francisco, although he never visited the town named for him. In 1888 the Phelps Dodge Company, represented by Dr. James Douglas, staked and developed claims adjoining the original Copper Queen claims. The two companies merged in 1885, making greater development and expansion possible. In spite of labor troubles, two world wars and ensuing depressions, Bisbee has hung on as an established city due to expert long-range planning and development by the copper companies. It started losing population immediately after the stock market crash of 1929 and dwindled from over nine thousand in 1920 to less than four thousand in 1950. During the 1940s Bisbee was plagued with a shortage of skilled labor, and this persisted even after World

War II. Conversion to open-pit mining took several years, up to 1951, when the Lavender Pit Mine was opened; and the Bisbee area population more than tripled by 1960.

Douglas was assured of permanency when the Copper Queen Mining Company build a smelter there in 1901, and a public utilities corporation was formed in 1902. The town was named for Dr. James Douglas, who had given technical advice on the construction of the smelter. Douglas grew rapidly until 1920 and has been fairly stable since that time. Copper smelting is still the largest industry in Douglas, but a few small factories add to the economy. The major agricultural crop is chiles which are processed in a small seasonal cannery.

Willcox was originally called Maley because the railroad which caused it to exist was built through the ranch of a man named Maley. The name was changed to Willcox almost immediately when General Orlando B. Willcox, Commander of the Department of Arizona, came through the town on the train in 1880. The town was built as a cattle shipping center and a trading center for the surrounding cattle ranches. More recently, irrigated acreage has been developed to grow lettuce, cotton and other cash crops. In addition, small grains are grown for pen-feeding cattle.

Fort Huachuca was established in 1877 and was of great importance as a military post until the surrender of Geronimo in 1886. The fort was relatively inactive until 1911, when it became headquarters for troops posted along the Mexican border to protect Arizona against raids during a Mexican revolt. It reached maximum importance during World War II when twenty-two thousand military and eight thousand civilians were stationed there. Since World War II it has been activated and deactivated several times, but became an electronic proving ground in the early 1950s and has every prospect of remaining a permanent and extremely important military establishment. Sierra Vista has grown around Fort Huachuca to provide off-post housing for civilian personnel. The military and civilian payrolls, as well as the expenditures for supplies, are of tremendous importance to the economy of Cochise County and the whole State.

The county seat is Bisbee and its elevation is 5,350 feet.

COCONINO COUNTY: Coconino County was formed out of the northwestern corner of Yavapai County on February 19, 1891, and named for the Coconino Indians. With an area of 11,886,720 acres, it is the largest county in Arizona and the second largest in the United States. The County is most famous for the scenic wonder of the Grand Canyon. Another one-third is privately owned. Nearly one-third of the total area is Navajo, Hopi, Hualapai, and Kaibab Indian reservation land, and the remainder is taken up by the Kaibab and Coconino National Forests and national parks and monuments, the largest of which is the Grand Canyon National Park. The highest mountain is Humphrey's Peak (12,670) in Coconino County. Flagstaff is the county seat.

The earliest settlements in what is now Coconino County were devoted primarily to cattle ranching, though Mormons attempted to start an agricultural settlement around 1873 at the site of the present Tuba City. Five years later the Mormon leader, Erastus Snow, laid out the present town site of Tuba City, and Mormons settled there to farm, not realizing it was on Navajo reservation land. About the same time, Mormons also attempted to start woolen mills at what is now Moenkopi. They expected that the Indians would furnish their labor supply, but the project was soon abandoned.

William Bass capitalized on the tourist value of the Grand Canyon when he discovered an Indian train into the Canyon and set up tent houses for guests. Bass also mined copper and asbestos and, when a branch railroad line was built to handle his ores, it brought tourists in large numbers. Tourism has remained a major economic factor. The construction of Glen Canyon Dam began in 1957 in the northeastern corner of the county. It has had, and will continue to have an important economic impact on the county. For a long time lumbering has been the chief industry of the county, as the area has an abundance of commercial grade trees.

Shortly after construction began on the Glen Canyon Dam in 1957, the city of Page was established to house construction and government workers and their families. Named for John Chatfield Page, Commissioner of Reclamation, 1937 to 1953, it has grown in to a fair-sized community.

Williams is the only early settlement in Coconino County besides Flagstaff that has maintained status as an incorporated city. The first two white men settled there in 1876 but sold out their interest the next year. The post office was established in June, 1881, and the coming of the railroad started Williams on its long history of prosperity to poverty to prosperity. It gradually became an important lumbering and railroad town and is known today as the "Gateway to the Grand Canyon."

GILA COUNTY: Gila County was formed on February 8, 1881 from portions of Maricopa and Pinal Counties. Its area was extended eastward to the San Carlos River by petition in 1889. Part of its southern boundary is Gila River, for which the county was named. It contains 3,040,000 acres, making it nearly equal in size to Graham County. The county seat was established at Globe and has remained there. More than one-half of the area in Gila County is occupied by the San Carlos Reservation, and almost all the rest of it is taken up by the Tonto National Forest. The only privately owned lands in the county are in a small rectangle surrounding the Globe-Miami district, and a slightly larger area in the triangle formed by the southern boundary. The federal government controls ninety-four percent of the land in the county.

Mining and livestock raising are the principal industries of Gila County. This will continue to be true, although the completion of State Highway 65, from Phoenix and over the Mogollon Rim, has made the Tonto Basin-Payson recreational area easily accessible to Salt River Valley residents. Many have summer homes in the area and a great many more drive up for weekend hunting, fishing, and camping.

Mining is the most important industry. The Inspiration Consolidated Copper Company and the Miami Copper Company have mines and smelters working near Globe and Miami, and construction of a complete mill and development of the mine at Christmas is going forward. There are three new asbestos mills in operation which, it is hoped, will attract manufacturers of asbestos products.

The oldest and most important community in Gila County is Globe, which grew into a community in 1875 after the first discovery of rich silver ores in the district had taken place in 1874. These discoveries were soon worked out, and Globe might have relapsed into oblivion if the Silver King Mine, twenty miles southwest, and the Stonewall Jackson Mine, twenty miles northwest, had not been discovered in 1875. Both of these were very rich and extensive locations. Globe was in a strategic place to benefit from both, as it already had a smelter and a good water supply. There was an immediate stampede of bonanza hunters creating the towns of Pinal City at the Silver King (population of 166 in the 1880 census), and McMillanville at the Stonewall Jackson Mine (population of 150 in the 1880 census). Pinal City was on the site of the Southwest Arboretum; no traces of it can be found today. McMillanville has two adobe shacks in very poor condition still standing among rusted pieces of roofing, mining machinery and faint outlines of foundations. The silver in the mines was worked out by 1885, and both towns were deserted by 1890. Globe, however, continued to grow because rich copper deposits were found there in early 1880s.

The development of the copper mines in the area expanded smelter operations and created mines in the area expanded smelter operations and created the town of Miami in 1907. The Inspiration Mine Company constructed a huge reduction plant there in 1909 which has led to Miami sometimes being called the "Concentrator City".

Although Globe is one of the state's oldest incorporated cities, it has not been incorporated continuously. It first incorporated in 1880, but sometime during the next twenty-five years the townspeople apparently forgot it was incorporated, for in 1905 they did it again. This time, citizens of Globe decided it was too expensive and disbanded their Articles of Incorporation. Finally, they incorporated once more in 1907 and have remained an incorporated city since.

Central Heights is a residential suburb of Globe, although not within the city limits. It was originally an area of mine owners' residences, closer to the mines than to the town and smelter.

Hayden was started in 1910 as a mill and smelter town for the mines in the southern tip of the county.

Winkelman is a shipping point for cattle for the various ranches in the valleys surrounding the junction of the Gila and San Pedro Rivers. It is expected to expand considerably when the mine at Christmas begins operation.

Principal industries: mining, livestock, tourism.

Points of interest: Salt River Canyon, Tonto National Monument, Coolidge Dam, Roosevelt Dam, Kinishbe Ruins.

County seat: Globe.

Elevation: 3,540 feet.

GRAHAM COUNTY: Graham County was created on March 10, 1881, from parts of Apache and Pima Counties. It is assumed that the county was named for Graham Mountains. Isadore Solomon started the county seat with his sawmill which was known as Solomonville; but, shortly afterward, the county seat was moved to Safford, where it stayed until 1883, when it was returned to Solomonville. After Greenlee County was split from Graham County in 1911, the county seat moved back to Safford, where it has remained. The present Graham County has an area of 2,950,400 acres. Three portions of the Coronado National Forest are located in Graham County, and approximately one-third of the county area is Indian reservation land.

Graham County began as an agricultural area, and agriculture has remained its primary economic base. Copper and lead mining have varied in importance to the county and are presently at a low level. However, some exploration is being conducted in the Safford area. Tourism is of importance, particularly in mountain resorts during the summer months.

A new Camp Grant was established in what is now Graham County when the unhealthy location of old Camp Grant in Pinal County and its unsavory reputation due to the massacre of Aravapai Indians there in 1871, caused the military to seek a more suitable location. The shift was accomplished either in later 1872 or in early 1873, and troops were shifted to the new Camp Grant from Camp Crittenden (in Santa Cruz County) as well as from old Camp Grant. The only census figure ever recorded for Camp Grant was 243 in 1880. The name was changed to Fort Grant in 1879, but the establishment was already losing its importance with Fort Huachuca becomoing the major post in Southern Arizona. The fort was abandoned in 1905.

Safford was the next settlement in what is now Graham County. In 1874 a group of farmers who had been living in Gila Bend and whose land was periodically washed out by the flooding Gila River, followed the river to find a better location and settled the first American colony of civilians by Joshua Bailey during 1874. The post office was established in March, 1875, in the store. Safford has remained primarily a farming community, though some copper and lead mining have developed and exploration of copper claims north of Safford is in progress now. Tourism has become fairly important in and around Safford, and the city has drawn numerous retired workers as permanent residents in the past few years. It has grown from a population of 173 in 1880 to nearly five thousand in 1960.

Camp Thomas was established in 1876 in the Gila River Valley to replace old Camp Goodwin where malaria was quite prevalent. It was located about twenty miles northwest of Safford and only about six miles east of the old Camp Goodwin. The camp developed slowly and was built by the soldiers themselves because the government, stung by the expensive abandonment of Camp Goodwin, would not provide funds. The name was changed to Fort Thomas in 1883. Funds finally became available in 1884. The surrender of Geronimo in 1886 reduced the need for the fort and it was abandoned in 1892. Fort Thomas is still an active community, but it has never incorporated and has remained fairly small.

The present town of Pima was originally settled by Mormons in 1879 and was named Smithville after the Mormon leader, President Jesse N. Smith. Malaria and outlaws caused many problems, but the residents preserved and maintained the community. The name was changed to Pima when the post office was established in August, 1880. Pima incorporated before 1940 and has been listed in each census since 1890. It is still an active community but has been losing population gradually since 1930.

Thatcher is another community which was settled by Mormons about 1882. The first town site was selected in 1883, but it was relocated on higher ground two years later. The name was chosen after a visit by the Mormon apostle, Moses Thatcher. The post office was not established until 1888. Thatcher was, as most Mormons settlements are, an agricultural community and has remained essentially that, although Eastern Arizona Junior College was established there in 1891. Thatcher grew rapidly in population through 1910 and has grown gradually since that time.

Principal industries: agriculture, livestock.

Points of interest: Mt. Graham, San Carlos Lake, Aravapai Canyon, Fort Grant, San Carlos Indian Reservation.

County seat: Safford.

Elevation: 2,900 feet.

GREENLEE COUNTY: Greenlee County was created in 1911 from the eastern part of Graham County. The county was legally created by an Act of the Twenty-fifth Arizona Territorial Legislature on March 10, 1909, but political difficulties between the parent county and the new county delayed organization of Greenlee into an active county until 1911. The county contains 1,199,360 acres and more than half of the county area is included in the Apache and Gila National Forests. The division between Graham and Greelee Counties was made along the same boundary line as the eastern boundary of the San Carlos Indian Reservation. The county seat is at Clifton, the oldest community. The county was named after Mason Greenlee, an early settler who made the first location in the Greenlee mining district near Clifton. He first came to the area in 1874, but was forced by Indians to leave. He returned in 1879 and stayed the rest of his life.

The early development of Greenlee County was due to mining, which is still extremely important in this area. Cattle raising is also a main industry, although copper production has increased since 1950 and the production of molybdenum has reached significant proportions since that time. Modernization of methods has reduced the number of employed in the mining industry.

Clifton began as a community in 1872 when a group of prospectors, including Charles Shannon, the Lezinsky brothers, and two others named Metcalf and Stevens, explored the area and established copper mines. Exceedingly rich ore had been discovered there by an army scout in 1869, but he was not able to develop it. It is believed that the town was named because of its location in the midst of towering cliffs, although there was an early-day prospector named Henry Clifton who traveled through the district prior to 1872. Backed by eastern capital, the Detroit Copper Company was organized to develop the claims at Clifton. Copper claims were located on Copper Mountain, the present site of Morenci, as early as 1881. The mining town was known as Joy's Camp at that time. It was changed to Morenci in 1881 when the Detroit Copper Company bought the claims and built a smelter. Arizona's first copper concentrator was built at Morenci in 1886.

The coming of the railroad into the area was a great boom to development. In 1883 the railroad was completed and Duncan was established as the railroad shipping point for mining in the Clifton-Morenci area, as well as a cattle shipping point for ranches in what is now Greenlee County.

Metcalf was the mining town for the Metcalf mining claims which were close enough to Clifton to use the smelter there. By 1915 the ores in the Metcalf area had played out and the town gradually died away. The Depression following World War I, and the depletion of high-grade ore in both Clifton and Morenci, brought hard times to the area and many moved away during the 1920s.

Though the town of Morenci shows a sixty-three percent loss in population since 1950, the actual loss for the area was only 1,483 or twenty-nine percent, as many Morenci residents merely moved to new housing constructed by Phelps Dodge Corporation in nearby areas listed as Plantsite and Stargo in the 1960 census. This population shift made possible the razing of the old houses in order to get at ore which, though worthless at the time Morenci was built, had become valuable due to the introduction of new mining and processing methods. Another factor in this loss of population in the Morenci area is the trend toward commuting. Many miners are settling their families in Safford and even in Lordsburg, New Mexico, and commuting to work in Morenci.

Principal industries: mining, livestock.

Points of interest: Coronado Trail, Hannagan Meadows, Blue River, Morenci open pit mines.

County seat: Clifton.

Elevation: 3,465 feet.

MARICOPA COUNTY: Maricopa County, lying in the southcentral part of Arizona, covers an area of 9.253 square miles of desert valley and low mountain ranges. The Tonto National Forest, with its 7,645-foot Four Peaks Mountain, the desert region in the southwest portion of the county, and the 1,300 miles of canals which crisscross the county's central portion, all contribute to the topographical diversity characterizing the county. It encompasses three Indian reservations—Salt River, Fort McDowell, Gila Bend— and a small part of the Gila River Reservation. The average temperature range is between 75 degrees and 104.6 degrees in summer and between 35 degrees and 64 degrees in winter, with the sun shining eighty-eight percent of the possible time. The average rainfall is 7.2 inches a year. Much of the county is used for agriculture, depending on a vast network of irrigation canals from the dammed Salt and Verde Rivers.

The primary cities in the county are Phoenix, Scottsdale, Tempe, Mesa, Glendale and Chandler. About eighty-fivepercent of the county's population and forty-seven percent of the state's population is contained within these coterminous areas. The airline service is provided by three transcontinental and six regional carriers providing both passenger and air freight service with approximately one hundred scheduled arrivals and departures daily from the Phoenix area. The Santa Fe and Southern Pacific Railroads offer railway connections for freight and, to a limited extent, passenger travel. The county is served by two national bus lines along transcontinental routes, and one main bus line operates within the metropolitan area of Phoenix. The outer portion of the central urbanized section of the county is served by another bus line which offers only service between the suburbs but not within the suburbs. Because of the geographic dispersion of major industry and wide location of workers, public transportation is inadequate. For those with their own transportation, there are over twenty-six miles of completed freeway within Phoenix linking the city with uninterrupted freeway travel from Flagstaff to Tucson (Interstate 10 and Interstate 17). The excellent highways throughout the county are a major factor in the county's becoming a regional warehousing and distribution center. These highways are main arteries vital to the warehousing and distribution firms. The area is serviced by ten transcontinental truck lines, four transcontinental heavy equipment haulers and three transcontinental automobile transporters. There are thirty interstate truck lines, thirty-nine intrastate truck lines, REA Express and United Parcel Service.

More than one thousand years prior to the coming of the white man, the ancient Hohokam Indians were diverting waters from the Salt and Gila Rivers and cultivating the fertile river valleys. Settlements of what is now Phoenix began in 1865, when a hay supply point for Camp McDowell was set up about four miles from the present center of Phoenix. Prior to World War II, agriculture, tourism, government and some food and fiber processing, stimulated by availability of irrigation water in the Salt River Valley, were the principal factors influencing growth in Maricopa County. During World War II, the U.S. government encouraged the establishment of a number of basic industries in the Valley. After the war, the production was maintained, and in 1956 the value of industrial output for the state exceeded the value of agriculture products. Industrial development has kept pace with the vigorous population increase, with manufacturing showing the greatest increase.

Agriculture has historically been a major component of the county's economic base, with the county currently encompassing forty-four percent of the state's cultivated crop land. Maricopa County is the state's largest single county producer in all major crop categories: cotton, alfalfa, cereal grains, lettuce, onions and sugar beets. The county is the third most important county in the U.S. in terms of agricultural output. At the same time, however, agricultural employment has been slowly declining since 1950, due to increased mechanization and consolidation of farms into larger, more efficient operations.

The tourist industry, which includes the services industry, is a major contributor to the county economy. Natural and man-made attractions in the area, together with the climate, have made the Valley a prime vacation spot for the state and nation.

The trade section of the economy is the largest employer in the Valley. The improvement of interstate highway transportation through the Valley, as well as the central location of Phoenix within the thirteen-state and northern Mexico market, have made the county a wholesale and retail distribution center. Population growth has been a major stimulus to the growth of the government sector. Government is the third largest employer including state, local and federal employees, many of whom are involved with education.

Principal industries: agriculture, light industry, tourism, government business, electronics and high tech.

Points of interest: Phoenix Art Museum, Heard Museum, Phoenix Zoo, Pueblo Grande prehistoric ruins, Arizona State University, Apache Trail, Arizona Temple, Desert Botanical Gardens.

County seat: Phoenix.

Elevation: 1, 117 feet.
Population: About 3-1/2 million

MOHAVE COUNTY: Mohave County is the second largest
county in Arizona. Its total area encompasses 13,403 square
miles of which 176 square miles is covered by water, supplying
the county with an estimated one thousand miles of shoreline
on navigable rivers and lakes. The county is bordered on the
north and the west by the states of California, Nevada, and Utah;
and three lakes, Havasu, Mohave, and Mead, help make up the
western borders along the Colorado River. Elevation ranges
from five hundred to eight thousand feet, with most of the ter-
rain classified as desert. The highest areas of the county are
covered by vegetation types, characterized as scrub oak and
pinon pine and Ponderosa pine in the high levels.

The climate of Mohave County is generally arid.
Kingman, at an elevation of 3,345 feet, has an average maximum temperature of seventy-six degrees and an annual minimum temperature of forty-six degrees. Humidity is low, and
precipitation averages about eleven inches annually. The higher
elevations of the county receive snow in the winter, and all of
Mohave County, like most of Arizona, is subject to wide cli-
matic extremes. In Kingman, for example, the lowest daily
minimum temperature occurs in January (31 degrees) and the
highest daily average is in July (98 degrees)

Kingman, the county seat, is the largest city in the county.
Lake Havasu City and Bullhead City, the other major towns,
are located on the Colorado River. Both freight and passenger
service on the Santa Fe Railroad are available at Kingman. Bus
transportation is furnished by Greyhound, Continental Trailways
and the Las Vegas-Tonapah-Reno Stage. Regular airline service is maintained from Kingman and Lake Havasu City by
scheduled flights to Phoenix, Las Vegas and Los Angeles. Local intrastate and interstate trucking service is available.

Historically, mining has formed the major base of Mohave County's economy. Mining towns rose virtually overnight and waned just as quickly as deposits of gold and silver were discovered and depleted. In the early 1960s, there began an interest in the copper-molybdenum deposits in the area. The Duval Corporation operates an open-pit mine at Ithicac Peak, north of Kingman. The Standard Copper Company is developing the Copper World Mine, and underground operation near Yucca, south of Kingman. The El Paso Mine has been completed and is being conducted to extract sand and gravel, stone and feldspar deposits.

The major agricultural pursuit in the county is the production of beef cattle. Sheep raising is also conducted, although on a much smaller scale. Crop production is limited, consisting primarily of feeder crops, especially alfalfa.

The manufacturing industry is a relatively new influence on the county's economy. McCulloch Corporation opened the first production facility in Lake Havasu City and has announced plans to concentrate future expansion in that area. Ford Motor Company established an automotive proving ground near Yucca and also anticipates expansion. The Midwest Wax Paper Company has established operations at the Kingman Airport.

In terms of employment, the largest section in Mohave County is government, followed by trades and services, in support of a growing tourist industry.

The outlook for Mohave County is generally one of continued growth with the growth at Lake Havasu City leading the way. Several new manufacturing plants are currently scheduled for Havasu city, and the service industry should continue to grow with the rapid increase in population.

The Kingman area should grow tremendously. Tourism, the city's primary industry, could increase as the area becomes better known.

Bullhead City and its surrounding area should also continue to grow. A large segment of Bullhead City's growth must be credited to part-time residents who establish houses and trailers along the Colorado River as recreational and holiday dwellings. Services is the primary industry, and this will grow as the area develops.

Principal Industries: mining, livestock, manufacturing, tourism.

Points of Interest: Colorado River, Lake Havasu, Hualapai Indian Reservation, Davis Dam, Hoover Dam, Grand Canyon National Monument.

County Seat: Kingman.

Elevation: 3,345 feet.

NAVAJO COUNTY: Navajo County, the fifth largest county in Arizona, is located in the northeastern part of the state adjacent to the Utah state boundary. Its 9,915 square miles extend in a fifty-mile wide stretch for approximately 225 miles. The Navajo, Hopi and Apache Indian Reservations constitute a large portion of the land area of the county. The Mogollon Rim divides the county into two distinct physiographic areas, the Colorado Plateau and a rugged mountainous area. The high plateau country in the northern part of Navajo County is arid and desert-like, abounding with mesas and smaller plateaus. The southern part of the county is a rugged mountainous area, heavily wooded with pinon, juniper and Ponderosa pine.

The climate of the region has extremes from limited rainfall in the northern half to heavy precipitation in the form of rain and snow in the southern mountain regions.

Approximately one-third of Navajo County's population is located in a strip that is traversed by the Santa Fe Railway and U.S. Highway 66 (Interstate 40). This strip lies just below Holbrook, the second largest city and the county seat. Other communities in Navajo County include Show Low, Snowflake,

Pinetop and Heber-Overgaard. There are also several smaller trading centers on the Indian reservations serving a rather widely dispersed Indian population.

Historically, Navajo County's economy has been based on grazing, forest products and transportation. During the past decade, however, there has been an increasing trend toward diversification of the county's economic base. The processing of forest products has expanded from primarily logging to include molding and millwork firms and a paper manufacturing plant. A garment manufacturing plant and development of tourist accommodations both on and off the Indian reservations, along with increased construction activity, have also been responsible for much of this diversification.

The current economy of Navajo County is relatively stable, with some seasonal effects due to weather. According to employment figures, the major industrial sectors of the economy are government, services, trade, manufacturing and transportation. Tourism along U.S. Highway 66 is more extensive during the summer months, and declines during the winter months, causing a subsequent decline in the services and trade industries. Manufacturing also exhibits a decline in employment during the winter months. This is because much of Navajo County's manufacturing, centered around wood products and logging activities which supply the mills with raw material, comes to a halt during the winters. There is also some seasonal employment in highway and railway maintenance, with substantial increases in the summer months.

Government employees are mostly federal, with the major agency employers being the U.S. Public Health Service, the Bureau of Indian Affairs and the U.S. Forest Service.

Principal industries: lumbering, agriculture, livestock, Indian crafts and trading, tourism.

Points of interest: Petrified Forest National Park, Painted Desert, White Mountains, Hopi Indian Villages, Navajo National

Monument, Monument Valley.
    County seat: Holbrook
    Elevation: 5,069 feet.

PIMA COUNTY: Pima County is one of the four original counties created by the First Territorial legislature on November 8, 1864. It was the home of the Pima Indians, a peaceful, agricultural tribe, for whom the county was named. The original county consisted of all Arizona south of the Gila River and east of Yuma County (almost all of the Gadsden Purchase). As the other counties were formed, Pima lost large portions to Maricopa, Pinal, Cochise, Graham and Santa Cruz; this left Pima with an area of 5,914,240 acres.

    A large section of Pima County is occupied by the Papago Indian Reservation. The small San Xavier Indian Reservation is also within its boundaries. It has two national monuments— both cactus forests—the Organ Pipe National Monument and the Saguaro National Monument. The Santa Catalina Mountains, north of Tucson, are a part of Coronado National Forest.

    Almost all industries existing in other counties of Arizona are also found in Pima County, with the exception of lumbering. Some lumbering was done in the 1870s in the Santa Rita Mountains, but it was not extensive. Tourism, trade, agriculture, educational developments, modern transportation and industrial developments are centered in Tucson, while mining is extensive in other parts of the county.

    The first known census of Tucson was taken August 6, 1820, giving a population of 384. The earliest recollections of a Tucson resident, born there in 1819, describe it as a Mexican military post of about ninety soldiers, about 140 adobe hovels without doors or framed windows, and a population of about three hundred people who farmed in the valley west of the town and cultivated fruit and vegetables which they sold to the government. The Mexican government never kept a large enough military establishment at Tucson to keep the Apaches under control, and Tucson could not grow. Even the farmland close to town was not sufficiently free from Apache raids and terror to provide a stable economy. In 1858 mail lines and a stage line were established, but the real growth of the town did not occur until some time after Arizona became a separate territory in 1863. Camp Lowell was established as headquarters of military administration for southern Arizona, enabling Tucson to become the outfitting and supply point for all trade in northwestern Mexico as well as southern and eastern Arizona. Trade with Sonora expanded rapidly, due to the fact that goods cost but little more delivered at Tucson than by water at Guaymas. At Guaymas the payment of customs and port duties was unavoidable, but goods arriving at Tucson could be packed in 100 to 150-pound packs and sent by mule train to all points in northern Mexico without payment of any type of taxes or duties. Tucson thus had a monopoly on trade with Sonora; this is the chief reason for its extremely rapid growth between 1866 and about 1900.

In 1861, Tucson, with a total of sixty-eight American voters, elected a delegate to the Confederate Congress; and this action made Arizona County of New Mexico Territory a part of the Confederacy. In June 1862, however, General Carleton's California Volunteers entered Tucson and officially returned Arizona County to the Union.

Hundreds and thousands of dollars were lost in the Ajo mines from 1861 to 1911 through poor management, lack of knowledge and deliberate swindles such as bogus reduction methods. In 1911 the Calumet and Arizona Company bought the properties, developed a permanent water supply, and invented processes for leaching the ore. The mine began intensified production in 1917. Ajo was reported in the census for the first time in 1920. In spite of the ups and downs of copper production and prices, Ajo has shown a continuous growth in each census report since.

Principal industries: mining, defense-oriented manufacturing, agriculture, tourism.

Points of interest: San Xavier del Bac Mission, Arizona-Sonora Desert Museum, Saguaro National Observatory, Organ Pipe Cactus National Monument, University of Arizona.

County seat: Tucson.

Elevation: 2,410 feet

PINAL COUNTY: Pinal County was created from parts of Maricopa and Pima Counties on February 1, 1875. At that time it included the rich Globe mining district, but in 1881 this area was lost to Gila County. Its present area is 3,441,920 acres. The origin of the name "Pinal" is lost; it could have been derived from the Pinal Apaches or from the pine groves in the high mountains. The county seat has been established in Florence since the formation of the county. Almost all of the Gila River and the Maricopa Indian Reservations and small portions of the Pima and the San Carlos Reservations are in this county. It also contains a portion of the Tonto National Forest. The history and economics of Pinal County are tied to the Gila River. Even today the river is of great importance for providing water, either directly or indirectly, for the widespread agriculture of the county, as well as being a part of its boundary. Rich agricultural districts throughout the center and rich mining developments in the northern and eastern mountains have characterized the growth of the county. New industries and developments within recent years are providing variety, including such diverse things as a baseball training camp, a steel mill and a large retirement community.

The earliest recorded settlement in Pinal County was Maricopa Wells with a population of fifty-three, first listed in the Census of 1860. It was important, as early as 1857, as a station on the San Antonio-San Diego mail route, the last place to get water before crossing the "Forty-Mile Desert" to the big bend of the Gila River. It is now the little community of Maricopa on the Maricopa Indian Reservation.

By the Census of 1870 two new town had sprung up in Pinal County: Adamsville in 1865 and Florence in 1868 (named by Territorial Governor Richard McCormick for his sister). Adamsville was a freighting and trading center on the Gila River, four miles west of Florence. It was the location of a flour mill, the only one between Tucson and California, and supplied many Arizona forts with flour. As Florence grew, Adamsville sank; the flour mill was moved and the town gradually disappeared. Florence developed as the center of the agricultural district of the upper Gila River. It later became a meeting point of stage routes to Prescott, Ehrenberg, Phoenix, Tucson, Yuma and the rich mining district of Silver King and Globe. The building of Coolidge Dam and the Ashurst-Hayden Diversion Dam on the Gila provided irrigation for the area, insuring its importance as an agricultural area. The Territorial Prison was transferred from Yuma to Florence in 1909, and it is the site of the state prison today.

In 1878 an extremely rich silver strike known as the Silver King, was made in the mountains nears present-day Superior. Very shortly, other mines and other towns sprang up in the district, none of which lasted beyond the life of the silver ores which were worked out by 1890. These were Silver King, Pinal City (see the history of Globe in Gila County), Silver Queen, and Reymert. The present town of Superior is at the location known as Silver King in 1880 and Silver Queen in 1882, as the community had no official name distinct from the mines. The town site of Superior was officially laid out in 1900 and named after the Arizona and Lake Superior Mining Company, the owner of the mines at that time. The Silver Queen proved more lasting than the Silver King because large underlying deposits of copper were found after the silver ore played out. On these, the community managed to stay alive until the Magma Copper Company bought the properties in 1910. The company developed and expanded copper mining in the area and built a large smelter at Superior in 1916, thus insuring its continuance.

Mammoth was the milling town on the San Pedro River set up to serve the old Mammoth Mine which was being worked for gold as early as 1873. The mine continued intermittently until 1901. In 1934 the mines were reopened to work molybdenum and vanadium, which in turn gave way to lead and zinc as ores in the mine and market prices varied. By 1952, the ores became leaner, lead and zinc prices dropped and inflowing water became a problem. The mines were closed and properties sold to the San Manuel Mine. Mammoth's existence today is dependent on the operation of San Manuel.

The original San Manuel locations were made in 1870, but there was no real development until 1944 after its commercial possibilities had been discovered by the exploration program of the U.S. Geological Survey and the U.S. Bureau of Mines. San Manuel was the first mine to use the active participation of government agencies in long-shot exploration for minerals. It took $100,000,000 and thirteen years' exploration, development, and construction to bring San Manuel into operation. Due to this outlay, however, Magma Copper Company has a thriving concern with a well-laid-out town of over four thousand population.

The copper deposits at Ray were discovered in the 1870s but were not continually and successfully developed until the Ray Consolidated Copper Company was organized in 1906. They developed the mines for working large tonnages of low-grade ore and built a smelter at Hayden. In 1933 the Ray Mines became a division of Kennecott Copper Corporation which continued to develop and expand operations contributing to the growth of Ray and Hayden. Since 1960 the town site of Ray has become a part of the open-pit mining operation, and the residents moved to the town of Kearny near Hayden. Sonora is the residential town for many workers in the Ray mines.

The coming of the railroad created the town of Casa Grande, so named because it was the closest town on the railroad to the Casa Grande ruins. It grew slowly as a cattle shipping point and agricultural center until recent years when it has expanded more rapidly due to the addition of new industries. Arizona City, a new community for retired people, is being completed and rapid growth is expected.

Coolidge and Eloy are both agricultural centers, coming into existence when the area was developed for farming in the 1920s. As cotton has become more important as a crop and more extensive areas have been irrigated, Coolidge and Eloy have grown to provide cotton gins, shipping and trading centers, and residential centers for farm workers.

Points of interest: Southwestern Arboretum, Superstition Mountains, Pinal Pioneer Parkway, Picacho Peak, Casa Grande Ruins National Monument, Central Arizona College, Historical County Seat, Arizona State Prison.

County seat: Florence.

Elevation: 1,500 feet.

SANTA CRUZ COUNTY: Santa Cruz County was a region known well to many Indian tribes which were its earliest inhabitants. In 1700 it was estimated by the Spanish that there were some five thousand natives populating the region. To these Indians it must have seemed like Paradise with its rolling hills and sheltered canyons, its abundance of wild game and its flowing streams.

From the early sixteenth century come reports of fair-haired visitors in the Santa Cruz Valley. Spanish conquistadores, possibly even the famed explorer Cabeza de Vaca, are said to have trekked across the region which is now southern Arizona.

In 1529 the Franciscan priest Fray Marcos de Niza entered the area near the site of what was to later become Lochiel. Venturing north into what is now northern Arizona in search of the mythical Seven Cities of Cibola, he returned to Mexico City with glowing accounts of the vast riches to be had. It was these reports that sent the Spanish nobleman and soldier, Francisco Vasquez de Coronado, on his fateful expedition the following year.

For almost another 150 years, no further attempt was made to again enter this land known to the Spanish as "Pimeria Alta". . . the upper land of the Pima Indians. In 1687, in an attempt to protect a land passage from Mexico to California through the establishment of missions along the route, Father Eusebio Francisco Kino was sent out to establish the first of what was to become a string of twenty-one missions in Sonora and southern Arizona. The mission at Tumacacori was established in 1691, after Padres Kino and Salvatierra were asked to the Indian village by special invitation.

The first permanent white settlement came into being in 1737, with the founding of the Spanish mission rancheria along the banks of the flowing Santa Cruz. Spanish attempts to pronounce the Papago name "Chuevak" came out as Tubac. Fourteen years later, in 1751, the Pima Indians rebelled, killing some one hundred people and destroying Tubac and many other missions in the region. It was this uprising that resulted in the establishment of the First Spanish Garrison in the north, the Presidio San Ignaicio de Tubac, built in 1752.

Little activity was seen again until 1758, when Father Garces was sent to the mission at San Xavier del Bac near Tucson. Garces, being an active man, soon began to explore the region. In 1771 he succeeded alone and on foot to cross the Yuma and California deserts and reached the base of the Western Sierras. Upon his return Garces' reports so fired the imagination of Captain Juan Bautista Anza of the Tubac Presidio that he offered to open an overland route to the mission and presidio that had recently been established at Monterey in California.

In 1794 Father Gutierrez arrived at Tumacacori, then head of the district. He found the church "split in two parts," almost in total ruin due to an Apache raid while most of the soldiers at Tubac were on the Anza expedition to California. His life work was to be the building of a new and larger church. Father Gutierrez died in 1820 and although it was never finished, the noble structure still stands as a national monument.

After the passing of Father Gutierrez, the lands were sold, villages and all, for a sum of only $500.00 to a governor of Sonora as "abandoned Pueblo lands." The intense winter of 1848-49 destroyed crops and stock, forcing the few remaining villagers of Tumacacori to finally give up and leave their homes to join kinsmen at neighboring San Xavier.

Falling to ruin, Tumacacori stood silent until 1907 when Will C. Barnes, then an assistant U.S. forester, suggested that Tumacacori mission be made into a national monument. In September, 1908, President Theodore Roosevelt proclaimed ten acres, including the church and most of the village site, the Tumacacori National Monument.

In 1822, after Mexico obtained its independence from Spain, restrictions upon Americans entering the region of Santa Cruz County were relaxed. The treaty of Guadalupe Hildalgo in 1848 ended a brief war with Mexico and it was the Gadsden Purchase of 1854 that put the entire region under the Flag of the United States.

The memories of tales of the Spanish "Bolas de Platas" beckoned mining men into the region. One of the first to arrive in the new territory was Charles D. Poston in 1856 as a member of the Sonora Exploring and Mining Company. The company took over the empty presidio at Tubac and set up its headquarters. As the little community grew, Poston opened a book of records, performed the marriage ceremonies, baptized the children and granted divorces.

As soon as it was known that an American company had arrived in Tubac, Mexicans from Sonora came in great numbers to work. Skilled miners could be employed for wages of fifteen to twenty-five dollars per month plus provisions. The Mexican senoritas that also came had a refining influence on the frontier population. . . many had been educated at convents and all were practicing Roman Catholics. They called the American men "Los God-Dammes" and the American women "Las Camisas-Coloradas."

However, in June, 1861, with mining machinery running smoothly, with the mines yielding handsomely, and with 250 employees working and being paid, activity in Tubac stopped. Because of the threat of Civil War, the post of Fort Buchanan, on the Sonoita Creek and at Tubac were ordered abandoned and destroyed. The settlers left and the prosperity of the entire region came to an end.

With the exodus of the United States Army, the Apaches swept across the land driving all but a few from the region. One hardy soul who remained was Pete Kitchen. He was called a "rough charcoal sketch of a civilized man," and to the wild Apache he was more terrible than an army with banners. His hacienda at the junction of the Santa Cruz River and Potrero Creek was as much a fort as a ranch house.

The frequent Indian raids killed and wounded Kitchen's employees, stole his stock and studded the skins of his pigs with arrows. In 1871 they killed his son, but the Apache was never able to make the determined Kitchen flee from the valley.

The route from Tucson south into Sonora became known as the way "from Tucson, Tubac, Tumacacori, to Hell."

The end of the Civil War brought back the soldiers and the Apache menace gradually faded away. Apache warfare ended completely in 1886. Although major mines had been discovered before the Civil War, the frequent Indian trouble kept the population and returns low. In 1867 Fort Crittenden was established, overlooking the site of abandoned Fort Buchanan in an attempt to protect the region.

The mining camps of Washington and Duquesne prospered in the 1890s with the extraction of lead, silver, zinc, and copper from the rich earth. One mine, Mt. Mowry near Patagonia, yielded about 1.5 million dollars in silver and lead ore during the period from 1859 to 1862. At one time there were 350 mining claims within a fifteen mile radius of Patagonia.

The cattle industry, originally introduced by the early Jesuit missionaries, expanded throughout the rich grazing ranges with their waist-deep grasses. To the Andalusian or Mexican Blackhorns of the padres were added Texas longhorns, then Herefords and almost every other known type of beef cattle.

Adding to the prosperity of the Santa Cruz Region came the railroad. Rumors that the railroad planned to make Calabasas the port-of-entry into Sonora brought an overnight tent-city. The first brick hotel in the territory was built. The *Tucson Citizen* reported that Calabasas had the "finest hotel west of the Rock Mountains, and ten or twelve of the best looking Boston-made girls." The Hotel de Santa Rita became known as a popular summer attraction for Tucsonians, so popular that a steamboat line via the Santa Cruz was promoted for a while. When the railroad chose to make Nogales its port-of-entry, the Calabasas tents silently stole away leaving only the prolific wild gourds growing in the area as they were when the first Spanish arrived.

In 1880 Jacob Isaacson, an itinerant peddler from San Francisco, built a small store at the border on the stage route from Tucson to Guaymas. The place which Isaacson picked had in the early days furnished shelter to travelers on the Kino Trail. With its walnut grove in the mountain pass, it was the custom camp at "Los Nogales." Isaacson lived alone, fighting off Apaches and serving the friendly Mexican ranchers and travelers.

In 1881 the Santa Fe Railroad sent out a party of surveyors to extend the line into Mexico. They stopped at the merchant's place which had become known as Isaacson or Isaactown. They made it headquarters and the name Isaacson was attached to the post office.

John Brickwood constructed the second permanent building in 1882, a saloon straddling the border making it possible to fix the revenuers by stepping out the back door to do business. This practice ceased in 1907 when a sixty foot by two mile "Public Reservation" was created by Presidential Proclamation.

The future of the border city, by then called "Line City", was assured in 1882 when the New Mexico and Arizona Railroad joined the Sonora Line. The day the railroad lines joined, two engines met at the border facing each other and the last spike, a silver one, was driven. The railroad called their new station "Nogales," which seemed to settle the name. The citizens petitioned to have the post office name changed from Isaacson to Nogales. In 1893 the town became incorporated.

In 1895 the growth of Nogales and the development of mines in the vicinity resulted in the necessity for greater communication between the area and its county government. However, at that time, being part of Pima County, one was forced to travel to and from the county seat in Tucson by way of the railroad through Sonoita and Fairbank, a trip taking almost a day. Thus came the demand for local government and the creation of a new county to be called Grant County. Finally on January 25, 1899, after some years delay, a bill for the creation of a county was introduced to the Territorial Assembly. On March 15, 1899, Santa Cruz County was established with Nogales chosen as the county seat. Nogales has an elevation of 3,800 feet.

YAVAPAI COUNTY: Yavapai County was one of the four counties created by the First Arizona Territorial Legislature on November 8, 1864. It originally included about half of the entire territory, but was divided repeatedly, so that now, all or part of nine of Arizona's present fourteen counties were, at one time, part of Yavapai. All but one of these nine counties are now larger than Yavapai, which has an area of 5,179,240 acres. The name Yavapai is from an Indian Tribe and Means "sun people." The county seat is Prescott, which was also the territorial capital from 1864 to 1867 and from 1887 to 1889. Almost half of Yavapai County is in national forests.

Yavapai County has long been famous for fabulous placers and mines as well as its lumber resources and stock raising areas. Tourism, in Prescott, Mingus Mountain, and the Verde Valley has become increasingly important in recent years with the completion of Black Canyon Highway. A large cement plant, providing cement for construction at Glen Canyon Dam, has aided the economy of the county. Other new firms recently started or planned include a pole-treating plant and a motion picture equipment and supplies manufacturing firm.

The only established community that has continued to grow through the years is Prescott. When the governor of the new Arizona Territory arrived at Fort Whipple in December 1863, he decided that the seat of the new government should be near the fort. Accordingly, the territorial capital was established on May 30, 1864, a few miles from Fort Whipple. It was named Prescott in honor of William H. Prescott, the American historian and authority on Aztec and Spanish-American history. Two things about the early community of Prescott made it unique in Arizona. It was built entirely of wood, and almost all of its inhabitants were Americans. It is believed to be the birthplace of rodeos, which grew out of the annual Fourth of July celebrations held every year since 1864.

Walker is the next town to be listed in the census (1880). It was the center of extensive mining operations between 1875 and 1890 in the Bradshaw Mountains. The rich Congress Mine was discovered in 1883, creating the town of Congress, and later the railroad established Congress Junction as an ore shipping point. With the working out of the richest ores and the drop in the price of silver, mining decreased and both Walker and Congress became ghost towns. Congress Junction still exists today as a very small shipping point for cattle.

Claims in the Jerome area were filed and mining was started as early as 1873, but true development of that area had to wait for the railroad. In 1883 the United Verde Copper Company built a road to connect with the railroad at Ash Fork in order to bring in smelter equipment. The town established by the mine and smelter was named Jerome in honor of Eugene Jerome of New York, treasurer of the company. In 1886 William A. Clark bought the properties and built a narrow gauge railroad connecting to Ash Fork. He developed and operated the United Verde Company very successfully in spite of fire that could not be put out in some of the tunnels.

In 1912 James S. Douglas, son of Dr. James Douglas of Phelps Dodge, and Major Pickrell became major stockholders in the United Verde Extension, the former "Little Daisy" claim. They and George Tener of Pittsburgh developed it, and it broke into a true bonanza of forty-five percent copper. Like all bonanzas, this was an extremely rich development as long as it lasted but was exhausted by the late 1920s. In 1919 the United Verde Extension built a smelter and smelter town named Clemenceau, but it died when the United Verde Extension ran out of ore. It was never listed in the U.S. Census.

Tremendous blasting in the Black Pit Mine in 1925 caused Jerome to start sliding downhill, literally and figuratively. The concrete jail skidded slowly three hundred feet across the highway and tumbled on its side below street level. Citizens of Jerome shored up the buildings, but the slump in copper prices in the 1930s spelled the end of Jerome as an important mining community. Today, Jerome is being preserved as a ghost town and museum center for tourists.

Clarkdale (named after William Clark, owner of the United Verde Mine) was established as the smelter town for the United Verde, Jerome Verde, and Verde Central Companies. With the closing of the mines, Clarkdale was expected to die. However, since the town was owned by the mining company, it was sold. The new owner kept it alive by converting it into a community for retired people until new industry gave it a new life. The Phoenix Cement plant was established in Clarkdale in 1958 and insured the continued existence of the community.

Principal industries: livestock, mining, tourism.

Points of interest: Smoki Museum, Granite Dells, Jerome Tuzigoot National Monument, Montezuma Castle National Monument, Montezuma Well, Camp Verde, Horse Thief Basin, Joshua Forest Parkway, Yavapai College, Prescott College.

County seat: Prescott.

Elevation: 5,410 feet.

YUMA COUNTY: Yuma is the most western county in Arizona. It is bordered on the west by California and on the south by Mexico. Yuma County is predominantly desert interspersed with rugged mountains, however, there is an abundance of arable land in the valley regions.

The warm, dry climate provides an extended agricultural season and year-round recreation. Temperatures range from the upper nineties to the lower hundreds from May through September, and from the low forties to the middle eighties the rest of the year. The average annual temperature is fifty-two degrees in the north and sixty degrees in the south.

The city of Yuma is located in the southwest corner of the county. Due to the twisting of the Colorado River and the unusual placement of the United States-Mexican border, California lies to the north of Yuma and Mexico lies to the west. Most of the city is situated atop a mesa which extends south from the Arizona-California border. The fertile valleys which surround the mesa form the nucleus of the county's agricultural land.

The earliest economic development of the area which now comprises Yuma County was based on mining and trade. Colorado River crossings near the sites of present-day Yuma city attracted travelers and miners. As the West became more populated, the military superceded mining as a major source of income. During World War II and after, government employment rose to prominence with the establishment of military testing and training facilities.

Today, agriculture, military installations, tourism, and light manufacturing form the economic base for Yuma County. Agriculture is by far the leading sector. Alfalfa, cotton, sorghums, and citrus are the most important crops. Average annual agricultural employment was 9,225 in 1969, and farm income has been in excess of seventy-five million dollars for the past five years. Two military installations contribute significantly to Yuma's well-being. Yuma Proving Ground, the world's largest military installation, is located thirty miles northeast of Yuma. The Marine Corps Air Station, outside Yuma, adds an additional dimension annually to the economy besides providing many civilian jobs. Tourism is another major source of income in the county. Although no recent estimates of income from tourism are available, large numbers of visitors come in the fall and winter months taking advantage of the mild climate and recreation. Service industries account for nearly ten percent of total employment. Manufacturing, although limited, does play an important role in the economy, producing photo equipment, textiles, and paper products.

Economic indicators point to a steady rate of economic growth. Per capita effective buying income, bank deposits, and retail sales have shown continuous growth. Most sectors of the economy anticipate a moderate growth in employment or will remain stable.

The best prospects for future economic growth in Yuma County lie in the areas of trade, services, and manufacturing.

Principal industries: agriculture, mining, cattle feeding, tourism, government business.

Points of interest: Arizona Western College, Yuma Territorial Prison.

County seat: Yuma.

Elevation: 138 feet.

LA PAZ COUNTY: Founded in 1983 it is the youngest of the fifteen counties. The county has an area of about 4,430 square miles. It takes its name from the first county seat for Yuma county. At one time the city of La Paz was a famous mining town. About 80 percent of the land in present day La Paz County is owned by the federal government.

Points of interest: Colorado Indian Reservation, Alamo State Park, Buckskin State Park, Parker Dam, Kofa Game Range.

County seat: Parker

We have all heard of ghost towns. In the fifteen counties of Arizona there are many ghost towns. The author wishes to call your attention to some south of Tucson which have a rich history of fun to visit and explore. You can visit Cerro Colorado, site of the gold mining of the 1850s; Arivaca, a semi-ghost town with some interesting buildings. Oro Blanco is a noted stage stop dating from the 1870s. Ruby is one of the better known ghost towns in all of southern Arizona. Helvetia, Greaterville, and Alto are also in the Tucson area and while they were not large towns, they played a significant part in Arizona's early history. If you want to really admire the pioneer spirit, then you must head farther west near Salome, Arizona. There you can find ghost towns like Harqua Hala, Swansea and Signal. These were lonely and barren little towns and about as western as they can be. You will have to admire the courage and the real American spirit of those pioneers who pushed west to live and die in those God-forsaken places.

Chapter Ten

MILITARY OUTPOSTS OF THE WEST

It is said that a wicked soldier died in Yuma and was consigned to the fiery regions for his manifold sins; but unable to stand the vigor of the climate, sent back for his blankets.

J. Ross Brown
Adventures in the Apache Country, 1864

Arizona was a hardship post for the military. Anyone who was sent to this land of sand and Gila monsters, was almost considered punished by his superiors. No one really wanted to serve here at one of the many posts. While some had the spirit of adventure, very few really wanted to chase and kill or be killed by the Indians. After all, what did one do at an army post in the summer time? The nights are long when the temperature zooms over a hundred degrees. It is difficult to sleep. Daytime temperatures were worse. It is true that some of the forts were located in northern Arizona where the temperatures were cooler. But the loneliness of a frontier was a difficult adjustment. Women were few and there really was little social life with the opposite sex. It was like being sent to Siberia. Women simply refused to come to live in Indian territory.

Hirum C. Hodge, writing in his book, *1877 Arizona as it*

Was, has this to say:

> Recognizing the fact that no community or country can ever enter upon its highest state of prosperity, refinement, or happiness without the aid and assistance of woman, Arizona and her citizens would welcome the advent of larger numbers of the true, the pure, the good, of the superabundant females of other portions of the Union, and would give them a welcome such as goddesses might envy.

Despite the cruel hardships of the area, the American soldier wrote many a glorious chapter in the unfolding of the West. His bravery and his cunning was well known to the historians of the West.

The Army posts paid a big role in the history of Arizona. Many of them are famous. Without them Arizona would never have survived. Their prime role was to defend the Americans from the attacks of the Indians, and this they did with fervor. In the early days of Arizona, they were probably better known as forts. To wit, we shall mention the better known ones.

Fort Apache, in the White Mountain country, has an altitude of six thousand feet. Its original name was Camp Ord. Founded in 1870, it was active until about 1924.

Fort Bowie was established in 1863 and for many years it was one of the most important posts in the territory, being surrounded by hostile Indians. It was the headquarters for General Crook and his negotiations with Cochise. In 1886 Geronimo surrendered near the Fort. It was abandoned in 1894.

Fort Mohave is on the Colorado River, 325 miles above Yuma. It was established in 1858 and abandoned when the Civil War began, but was reopened a few years later to protect the local citizenry and closed permanently in 1890.

Fort McDowell, located about fifty miles east of Phoenix, was opened in 1865, and was renamed after General Irvin McDowell. It was from here that one of the early founders of Phoenix, John Y.T. Smith, carried on a hay business. The fort closed around the year 1890.

Fort Yuma is located in Yuma, and of all the forts, it must be considered the most strategic. In 1850, Major S.P. Hintzelman came to the Yuma site and was stationed at Camp Independence on the eastern bank of the Colorado River. The arrival of these soldiers was the beginning of Fort Yuma. The army leader called his camp Fort Independence, but by March, 1851, the troops had moved to the area of the old Spanish mission, and this place was soon named Fort Yuma.

Had it not been for the army establishing Fort Yuma at the confluence of the Gila and Colorado Rivers, doubtless the history of this country—in fact, the history of the entire west— might have been vastly different. The Indians would never have allowed the white settlement to remain, neither would they have allowed the thousands of immigrants to cross the desert of their domain unmolested. During the early history of the tiny white settlements, the Indians did rise up on occasion and kill or drive the inhabitants out, including the soldiers. It was only after the army garrisoned the fort with a large force that the Yuma Indians ceased resistance.

In 1986, the old army depot in Yuma, nearly 120 years old, was added to the state's parks system. It once doubled as a family home and office for the National Weather Services. The site, now known as the Army Quartermaster Depot, over the years was also known as a military-supply storage site and was a post for the International Boundary Commission. The park provides live representations of what life was like near the confluence of the Gila and Colorado Rivers during ten periods between 1500 and 1912.

The Army built the Quartermaster Depot in 1864 to serve

as a supply warehouse for goods destined for Arizona, New Mexico, Nevada, Utah and Texas. Goods arrived on paddle steamers and were unloaded and stored in the adobe structure. It was a very busy place and hired as many as seventy civilians.

Presently Fort McDowell is being reconstructed according to the 1879 plan at Pioneer, Arizona, an educational center where Arizona's pioneer heritage lives daily. Reconstruction is currently in progress. This historical museum, with twenty-seven buildings, including a blacksmith shop and original homes from the era of 1860 to 1890, is located about seventeen miles north of Phoenix on Interstate 17 and is open daily except for Christmas Day.

Chapter Eleven

FAMOUS ARIZONA GOVERNORS

Evan Mecham (1986-1988)

After 12 years of Democratic rule under Democratic governors, Evan Mecham, a Republican and a Mormon, was elected governor of Arizona in 1986. The first automobile dealer to ever hold this high office, ee was born on May 12, 1924, in Duchesne, Utah. He is married and is the father of seven children. He attended Arizona State University, was a fighter pilot in WW II, and was a prisoner of war in Germany for 22 days. He was elected to the state senate in 1960. In 1962 he lost an election to the U.S. Senate to Carl Hayden who was to serve in Congress longer than any other citizen in our history. In 1964 he ran for governor and lost to Democrat Sam Goddard. He ran again in 1974, 1978, 1982 and in 1986, he won with only 40 percent of the vote. One of his first acts was to rescind the Martin Luther King holiday in Arizona. Among many reasons given, the governor did not think that King deserved a paid holiday in Arizona. This opened a long debate in political circles. After a short time in office, he was facing recall, impeachment from office and a criminal trial. As time went on he managed to offend the Blacks, the Jews, women, Hispanics, Orientals and the news media. Many of his political appointees had dubious qualifications and he attacked the "establishment." He was finally impeached and Rose Mofford became governor on April 5, 1988. She was the first woman governor in Arizona history. Of all the politicians that held high office in Arizona, Evan Mecham holds a unique place.

Trivia About the Impeachment of Evan Mecham

Total Cost: Nearly $2 million
Defense Legal Fees: $300,000
Prosecution Legal Fees: About $350,000
Pages of Trial Transcript: 5411

Rawghlie Clement Stanford (1937-1938)

Stanford was born in 1878 in Buffalo Gap, Texas, arriving in Arizona in 1991 and working as a miner and as a cowboy. He served as a volunteer in the Spanish American War. As a self-educated lawyer, he gained the esteem of his fellow citizens and was elected a Maricopa County judge. As governor he was involved in three special sessions in 1937, battling for a revision of the sales tax. The mining companies were fighting to starve off the hike. Other controversies involved the highway patrol and an alleged Governor's Relief Fund. Stanford later served as a member of the Arizona Supreme Court. He died in 1968.

Thomas E. Campbell (1919-1922)

Campbell, nicknamed "Traveling Tom," was a native of Prescott and the first native-born Arizonan to serve in the legislature, serving first as assessor of Yavapai County and as a state tax commissioner before becoming governor. He is the only governor in the history of Arizona who served one year without pay (1916), because the election was contested. He made another bid for the governor's chair in 1936 but failed. He died in 1944.

Jack R. Williams (1967-1998)

A popular radio announcer and executive in Phoenix, Jack Williams became the fifth Republican governor by defeating Sam Goddard in the 1966 campaign. In 1970 he became the first four-year governor in the history of the state after the legislature lengthened the terms of some of the high state officials. He was embroiled in controversy after signing a disputed Farm Labor bill. Known for his conservatism, he took great pride in fiscal responsibility and maintained budget surpluses each year. He served as mayor of Phoenix from 1956 to 1960, and died in Phoenix in 1998.

Bruce Babbitt (1978-1986)

Babbitt assumed office after the death of Governor Bolin. The son of a prosperous family in Flagstaff, he received a geology degree from Notre Dame University, a masters degree in geophysics from the University of Newcastle in England, and a law degree from Harvard University. He was a strong contender for the Democratic nomination for the presidency in 1988. As governor he left a strong legacy of vigorous leadership and set an active tone of success.

Fife Symington

Fife Symington, the nineteenth governor of Arizona, was inaugurated on March 6, 1991, after winning an unprecedented special runoff general election. His gubernatorial campaign was founded on a commitment to bring Arizona fiscal responsibility, education reform, and environmental protection.

Symington was born in New York City on August 12, 1945. Raised in Maryland, he comes from a prominent political family. Symington attended Gilman Country Day and earned a Bachelor's Degree in Liberal Arts from Harvard University in 1968. As a Harvard student, he was an active supporter of Barry Goldwater's 1965 presidential campaign.

Symington was first introduced to Arizona in 1968, when he was assigned to Luke Air Force Base as a United States Air Force Second Lieutenant. He served as governor until 1997.

Rose Perica Mofford

Folks in Mofford's home town of Globe recognized the qualities of leadership and responsibility in this Arizona native at an early age. From seventh through twelfth grades, she was president of her class. She attained scholastic honors that have not been duplicated in more than four decades. In her senior year, she was voted "most outstanding" student and chosen class valedictorian.

Rose Mofford also excelled as an athlete. She earned All-American status as a member of the amateur Cantaloupe Queens softball team, and she twice has been inducted into the Arizona Softball Hall of Fame: first, for her performance on the field and, more recently, for her increasing support of youth and sports. She also made her mark as a basketball player, turning down a professional contract to join the All-American Redheads.

Instead, this versatile young woman left Globe for Phoenix to begin an amazing career in state government that now spanned 43-plus consecutive years. A national prize-winning typist, Rose started as a secretary in the Arizona Treasurer's Office, moved on to the Tax Commission, and then worked for a time as business manager of *Arizona Highways* magazine before commencing a 22 year stint as Assistant Secretary of State.

In 1975, Rose accepted the position as Assistant Director in the Department of Revenue in charge of administration. However, when Wesley Bolin succeeded Governor Raul Castro in the fall of 1977, it was a foregone conclusion that Rose Mofford would be appointed Secretary of State as Bolin's successor.

Ingenuity, efficiency and reliability were Mofford's contributions to the system. She computerized the immense filing and records in her office and cross-trained all employees. Today, the Secretary of State's office is regarded as a model of efficiency, while retaining that human—that "Mofford"—touch.

She won election to her first full term in 1978, and it was little wonder that she then won reelection by an overwhelming margin in 1982, leading in all 15 counties.

Rose Mofford's office became a prime tourist attraction to the Capitol building. Her collection of exquisite Kachinas is considered one of the finest in the United States. Coupled with an array of antique guns and valuable southwestern artifacts, the collection has turned her seventh floor "museum" into a "must" stop for countless visitors.

Rose continued her education throughout her career, attending Phoenix College and the U.S. Defense Industrial College, where she graduated with perfect scores. She also attended sign language classes so she could communicate with the hearing impaired. The Cystic Fibrosis Foundation named her "Humanitarian of the Year" in recognition of her dedication to humanity. The Arizona Retarded Citizens presented her with the "A.R.C. Public Service Award" and through her efforts, the capitol Christmas tree was decorated with A.R.C. handmade decorations. She was a member of the Board of the Mercy Care Foundation and was recognized by the Arizona Association of Industries for distinguished service to the people of Arizona. She was the recipient of the "Distinguished Public Servant and Dedicated Humanitarian" award from St. Jude's Children's Research Hospital and recipient of the American Red Cross 1987 Arizona Heritage Award.

Rose was a member of the Advisory Board of the Liberty Bank, Honorary Founder of the Benevolent Protective Order of the Elks, Honorary Board of Director on the Crime Prevention League, member of the Alcoholism Council of Tucson (A.C.T.), Board Member of the National Council on Alcoholism, Vice Chairman of the Diamond Jubilee Commission and served as a member of the Board of Trustees for the Lion's Sight and Hearing Foundation and its Permanent Trust Fund. In her own words, "I'd sew for orphans, teach crafts—anything that would touch people's lives."

"Aunt Rose," as she is affectionately called by her friends, elevated the level of women's expectations in government service. As president of the prestigious National Association of Secretaries of State, she turned a social organization around to business which has been carried forward by her successors. She was the first woman elected as director of the Central Arizona Water Board in 1976. She served on the advisory board of the National Council on Alcoholism. She was named Honorary Member of the Glendale Optimist International Club, the first woman to ever receive this honor and on October 30, 1986, Rose was unanimously approved as an Honorary Member of the Arizona Boys State Board of Directors in appreciation of her valuable assistance over the years.

Rose wholeheartedly supported the needs of the Assistance League, Veterans of Foreign War Auxiliary, Business and Professional Women's Clubs, Foundation for the Blind, Freedom Foundations at Valley Forge, Soroptomist Club, Arizona Women's Commission, Fraternal Order of Eagles, and the Arizona Cattle Growers Association. She was chairman of the U.S. Savings Bond Drive for the fourth year, past chairman of the United Fund, Cancer Drive, Red Cross, and many other civic and community projects such as the Executive Board of the Arizona State Employees Credit Union, Arizona Girls Ranch, 4-H Clubs, VICA, Arizona Arthritis Foundation, Boys and Girls State, and Plus Sixty Personnel, to name a few.

Although Rose attributed the success of her office to the diligent dedicated staff, the energy and vivaciousness of the Secretary of State are regarded as key ingredients. "I've seen her stop everything to help someone with a problem," an admiring employee said, "that's something you don't see officials do very often."

A native of Arizona, Rose realized the importance of the resources of all 15 counties in our beautiful state and attributed much of her success to the values she learned growing up in a rural setting.

Jane Dee Hull

Jane Dee Hull became the twentieth governor of the State of Arizona on September 5, 1997.

Prior to becoming Governor, Hull was the sixteenth Secretary of State since Statehood, talking office on January 3, 1995. She was the first Republican to be elected to the office since 1931.

Hull began her career in public office in 1979 when she was elected to represent District 18 in the Arizona House of Representatives.

In 1989, Mrs. Hull was chosen by her fellow representatives to serve as the first woman Speaker of the House. She had previously served as House Majority Whip and Chairman of the Government Operations Committee. Her final year in the legislature, Hull served as Chairman of the Economic Development Committee, as well as the Ethics Committee. She also served as Speaker Pro Tem.

Hull holds a Bachelors Degree in Elementary Education from the University of Kansas and did postgraduate work in Political Science and Economics at Arizona State University. She is also a graduate of the Josephine Ethics Institute.

She serves on the boards of numerous community and service organizations.

Jane Dee Hull and her husband, Terry, a semiretired obstetrician, have four children and eight grandchildren.

Chapter Twelve

ARIZONA CONGRESSMEN
AND THE EXECUTIVE BRANCH

The land taken over in the Gadsden Treaty in Arizona was so desolate, deserted and God-forsaken that a wolf could not make a living upon it.

Kit Carson

The Arizona delegation to the United States Congress is an extraordinary one with very capable and distinguished lawmakers. Two of the present members have national reputations and Arizona can be proud of its outstanding representation in Congress.

John McCain

McCain is a Republican senator who took office in the U.S. Senate on January 1, 198 replacing Senator Barry Goldwater. He was born on August 29, 1936, in the Panama Canal Zone. Senator McCain is a graduate of the Naval Academy and a former Navy pilot. In Vietnam he was a prisoner of war for five years. His father and grandfather were admirals in the Navy. The Senator retired from the Navy in 1981 as a captain. After being in Arizona a very short time, he won a seat in Congress in 1982 and again in 1984. His campaign for the U.S. Senate took in more than two million dollars. His political ideology follows President Reagan and President Bush although occasionally he votes the other way. He expects to be a candidate for the White House in the year 2000.

Bob Stump

Congressman Stump was born in Phoenix on April 4, 1927 attending elementary school in Phoenix and high school in Tolleson. He attended Arizona State University and received a degree in agronomy in 1951. During World War II he served in the U.S. Navy. Mr. Stump has for many years been a cotton and grain farmer in the Tolleson, Arizona, area. In 1958 he was elected to the Arizona House of Representatives where he served for eight years, two as president of the Senate (1975 and 1976). Stump has three children: Karen, Bob and Bruce. He was elected to his first term in the U.S. House of Representatives in November of 1976. A Republican, Congressman Stump represents District Three.

John Kyl

Kyle, a Republican Senator who represents District Four., was born on April 25, 1942, in Oakland, Nebraska, and he received his Bachelors and law degrees from the University of Arizona. He is married and has two children. Congressman Kyl is a fiscal conservative and follows President Reagan's ideology. He was a partner in the law firm of Jennings, Strouss and Salmon.

Jim Kolbe

Republican Congressman Kolbe is from District Five, and was first elected to Congress in 1984. He was born on June 29, 1942, in Evanston, Illinois, and received his bachelors degree in political science from Northwestern University and his masters degree in business administration from Stanford University. He served in the U.S. Navy in Vietnam and was discharged in 1969. He served in the Arizona Senate for three terms.

Ed Pastor

A native Arizonan, Ed Pastor was born in Claypool, Arizona, on June 28, 1943. He earned his juris doctorate in 1974 and bachelor of arts degree in chemistry in 1966 from Arizona State University.

Pastor was elected to the Maricopa Board of Supervisors in 1976 and took office in January 1977. He was reelected in 1980, 1984, and 1988, but resigned on May 6, 1991, to run for Congress.

He was elected to represent the people of the Second Congressional District on September 24, 1991. He serves on the Committee on Small Business, Education and Labor and the Select Committee on Aging.

John Shadegg

John Shadegg was elected to represent Arizona's Fourth Congressional District in 1994. He has rapidly established a reputation in the Congress as a leading advocate for reduced government spending, a balanced budget and the reestablishment of state and individual rights. He serves on the Budget Committee, the Resources Committee and the watchdog Government Reform and Oversight Committee.

A native Arizonan, Shadegg was born October 22, 1949 in Phoenix, Arizona to Stephen and Eugenia Kehr Shadegg. He married Shirley Lueck in 1979. They have two children, Courtney and Stephen.

J.D. Hayworth

Congressman J.D. Hayworth represents Arizona's Sixth

Congressional District in Washington, D.C. He is serving his second two-year term in the U.S. House of Representatives.

J.D. serves on the House Ways and Means Committee, the first representative from Arizona to be appointed to this important post. The Ways and Means Committee is responsible for all tax-related legislation, as well as issues involving trade, Social Security and Medicare. J.D. also serves on the Veterans' Affairs Committee, and is an assistant whip in the leadership organization.

During his first term in the House, J.D. sponsored legislation which preserves Saddleback Mountain near Scottsdale, as well as a bill which expands the Walnut Canyon National Monument near Flagstaff. J.D.'s legislation to aid the Alpine Elementary School District in obtaining federally-controlled land for additional school facilities has also been signed into law.

Furthermore, in his first term, J.D. founded and chaired the Constitutional Caucus, and sponsored the "Congressional Responsibility Act," which improves accountability in the legislative process.

For his efforts, *National Review* magazine listed J.D. as one of the top ten conservative newcomers to Congress.

Prior to his election to Congress, J.D. was a public relations consultant, an insurance agent, and a radio news commentator. His media career included both radio and television, most notably seven years as a sports anchor on channel 10 in Phoenix.

A member of several local Republican organizations, J.D. is a Paul Harris Fellow of Rotary International. A member of the North Scottsdale Baptist Church, he serves as a volunteer reader for various community groups, is a speaker for D.A.R.E. and is also active in scouting, having earned the Eagle Scout Award.

J.D. goes home almost every weekend to his Arizona district, meeting with constituents and spending time with his family. District Six, one of the largest geographically in the nation, includes the northern and eastern portions of Maricopa County. It stretches to Pinal County in the south, Utah in the north and New Mexico in the east.

Hayworth earned a bachelor's degree, cum laude, from North Carolina State University in speech communications and political science in 1980.

Hayworth and his wife Mary have three children and are residents of Scottsdale, Arizona.

Chapter Thirteen

THE COLORADO RIVER

The first territorial legislature convened in 1864 and created four original counties for Arizona, one of which was Yuma. It was named for its chief Indian inhabitants, the Yuma tribe, who built huge, smoky fires to induce rain and they used the word umo which means smoke.

Pat Sievers, Historian

If there ever was a river that controlled the destiny of a state, it was and is the Colorado. The pages of Arizona history are filled with stories about the Colorado.

The total length of the river is about 1450 miles and it has about nineteen major canyons in its course. It was so big and so powerful that the story of Arizona in many ways was the story of trying to control this river.

Arizona and California fought for years over water rights to this great bonanza.

Just before the Civil War, the population of southern Arizona increased to such an extent that the problems of feeding the people became serious. During this period of early growth, most of the food was brought from the Pacific Coast at an enormous cost. Much of the food also arrived spoiled because of the lack of refrigeration. It became apparent to all that more food could be raised if there was more agricultural land. This meant more diffusion of water resources for a greater agricultural area.

There were many elaborate schemes at that time to bring water to the desert. One of the best plans was that of a certain Doctor Oliver Wozencraft, who worked out a scheme to irrigate and colonize lands in the Imperial Valley in California which is composed of the rich alluvial soil laid down by the Colorado River. Many of his ideas spread to Arizona.

To irrigate this potentially fertile desert on both sides of the Colorado, it was necessary only to turn a part of the Colorado. For with the river riding higher than the Valley, with already established channels coursing through the desert, the water would run from the river to the valley of its own accord. Doctor Wozencraft thought of the proposition which involved a diversion of water from the Colorado River toward the west into the region drained by the Alamo River which, in turn, would be distributed to points in California. From these places it could be distributed by a canal system.

To carry out Wozencraft's idea, the Federal Government was asked to grant the state of California some three million acres of land. The California legislature approved the idea, but the U.S. Congress failed to pass the necessary legislation. The reason for Congressional disapproval was that part of the canal system to be constructed would have to be located on Mexican soil. Seventeen years later, in 1876, a survey was made to determine whether or not it would be feasible to reach the Imperial Valley without following a route through Mexico. The report of the American engineers indicated that it would be unfavorable to build the canal entirely in the U.S., and again called attention to the natural route through Mexican territory.

This news was rather discouraging to those desiring to have water supplied to the desert in a canal located throughout its entire length on U.S. soil, but efforts to develop irrigation continued, although on a smaller degree than was suggested by Wozencraft. Large scale or modern irrigation did not begin until near the end of the century, although various small enterprises were tried, as well as numerous private endeavors.

Wozencraft, born in Ohio and educated in medicine in Kentucky, first came to the Colorado desert by way of Yuma on his way to the California placers in 1849. In the desert crossing, several of his party nearly collapsed and Wozencraft set off on his own in search of water. He must have been standing on the banks of Alamo Barranca, where it crossed the boundary from Baja, California to swing north toward the sink, when he got his great idea. "It was then and there that I was first convinced of the idea of the reclamation of the desert," he later wrote.

The real history of irrigation of modern Imperial and Yuma Valleys began in 1892, when engineer Charles Rockwood took preliminary steps in making large scale plans to irrigate the land with water brought from the Colorado River. As a result of Rockwood's efforts, the California Development Company was founded. The chief promoter of this firm was Colonel Ferguson. He induced J.W. Shenk, editor of the *Omaha Christian Advocate*, to invest $10,000 in the company. This event took place in 1899. One year later a hydraulic engineer, George Chaffey, discovering that water could be brought from the river more cheaply than had been anticipated. So he also invested in the California Development Company. In April, 1900, work was started on the canal system and the intakes in order to bring water to the firm's lands, some sixty miles west of Yuma in the Imperial Valley. The first water was delivered in June, 1901. Before long an agricultural boom had started. At the end of the fourth year, the Shenk family sold out part of their original holdings for $45,000.00, and the remaining portion brought another $40,000.00 several years later. This was quite a profit on an original investment of $10,000.00.

Like many other business enterprises, the California

Development Company encountered its share of troubles. The first setback came when an agent of the U.S. Department of Agriculture began to write most discouraging articles about the soils in the Valleys. Circular number nine was issued by the Bureau of Soils in 1902, stating:

> Aside from the alkali, which renders the soil practically worthless, some of the land is so rough from the gullies or sand dunes that the expense of leveling it is greater than warranted by its value. In the 108,000 acres surveyed in the Imperial Valley area, twenty-seven percent are sand dunes and rough land—the remainder of the level land, or fifty-one percent, contains too much alkali to be safe except for resistant crops.

In the meantime the Development Company was having internal disorder. Not only that, in 1906, the Colorado River suddenly abandoned its old-time bed to the Gulf of California and headed northwest into the Salton Sea. For the next twenty months, three unsuccessful attempts were made to get the river back into its regular channel. Finally a fourth endeavor resulted in the water's flowing again in its old course to the Gulf.

Now more and more people were coming into the vicinity around Yuma and the Imperial Valley. Most of those went south and southwest of Yuma. As additional land came under cultivation, more water was needed and after several experiments, it was decided that the best place to construct new canals from the Colorado was south of Yuma. The soil here was more desirable from a seepage standpoint, but unfortunately the site where the proposed new canals would be located belonged to Mexico.

After much discussion about water rights and maintenance of the canal, the Mexican government agreed to permit the construction through the desired territory, and the American farmers agreed to finance all costs and supply machinery needed to dig the artificial river bed. In return, they were to receive one-half of all the water which flowed through the canal. The Mexican farmers who in reality were American landowners, were to have the other fifty percent of the water going through the canal at a cost to be fixed by the Mexican government. Later the rate proved so inadequate that, although the amount of water used there over a period of years averaged more than a fourth of the total carried, the amount of money paid to the canal owners did not meet so much as one-eighth of the expense of maintaining that portion of the project in Mexican territory.

Sometimes the Colorado River has a heavy flow of water, then again, a smaller amount comes down the river. When the rain falls high up in the mountains and the snow melts, the water comes rushing down the mountain in torrents and fills the dry creek beds.

This is what happened when the floods came to Imperial Valley in 1905-1907. The Colorado River overflowed its banks and almost destroyed the cities of Imperial Valley.

In 1906 Imperial Valley was in great danger from floods. Water was everywhere. There was no transportation except by mule or wagon, and there was constant danger of dropping into a hole or ditch as roads had been washed out. Stores were flooded and adobe buildings slowly melted away. People tried to mend the levee by putting sandbags and brush in the opening to stop the flow of water. Finally there were no more sacks to fill with sand. The merchants opened sacks of sugar, flour, etc., and dumped the contents on the counter and used these sacks for sandbags. The men worked steadily at the levee and the wives and daughters brought them food as they stood knee deep in the water. The people had no place to rest as the water was everywhere.

The people of the Valley were aware of the danger and

they decided that something must be done to control the Colorado River. This disaster must not happen again. The people of the Valley must have water for irrigation, but it must be a dependable steady flow of water.

After studying the problem and gaining all the information possible, it was decided that Hoover Dam should be built to control the flow of water.

The first thing to decide was the location of the dam. The first decision was that the dam should be built in Boulder Canyon. Because it was learned that an earthquake fault was there, the engineers decided to move downstream to Black Canyon. It was first called Boulder Dam because of the location in Boulder Canyon. Later, the name was changed to Hoover Dam in honor of Herbert Hoover, our president at that time.

Construction of Hoover Dam started in 1931 and was completed in 1935. It was the largest dam to be built at that time. We now have some larger ones, but Hoover Dam is the highest dam in the Western Hemisphere.

Hoover Dam is the important dam for water control and regulation as far as Yuma Valley is concerned. This dam controls floods and stores water for irrigation, municipal, and industrial uses. It is also used for hydroelectric power.

The people of Yuma Valley depend upon the water stored in Lake Mead, the reservoir of Hoover Dam, to irrigate their land. This water is also used by the people of Mexico to irrigate their land. One main purpose of the dam is to supply the farmers with a steady flow of water when they need it. Before the dams were built farmers had too much water or too little or not any at all.

Another dam in Arizona, called Parker Dam, is just 150 miles from Hoover Dam. As Hoover is the highest dam, Parker is the deepest. It stores water to be supplied for the people of Los Angeles and other coastal cities, and protects the people downstream from flash floods of the Bill Williams River. Work was begun on this dam in 1934, and it was finished in 1938.

Another dam was built 148 miles downstream from Parker Dam and was named Imperial Dam. It is not used for water storage, but to divert water into the All-American Canal. Another purpose is to remove silt from the water. The silt must be taken out so that the canals will not get filled up and have to be dredged. Construction on this dam began in 1936, and six years later it was finished.

Laguna is another dam built in Arizona. The contract for building the dam was let to J.G. White and Company on July 6, 1905, and operation began on the 19th of the following month. In August, 1906, the contractors petitioned relief from their contract, stating that they were meeting with excessive costs. Several adjustments were made but when the contractors again petitioned for relief, the work was ordered taken over by the Reclamation Service on January 23, 1909, by force account, under the direction of the engineers of the Reclamation Service.

When finally completed, the dam was almost a mile long and raised the water ten feet from its natural elevation. The cost of the project up to 1910, including dam, levees and canals was $4,120,000.00, or about fifteen dollars for each acre that was expected to be irrigated in the future. A water user's association was formed and each member was to pay on the basis of number of acres irrigated. Eventually the project was to be self-liquidating. Laguna Dam has been a huge bonanza to the farming area of Arizona. Its untold benefits in dollars and cents to the average farmer's yield is incalculable.

The waters that once brought disastrous floods to the basin of the Lower Colorado River now make these acres very fertile. Millions of people depend upon the Colorado River and its dams for hydroelectric power for industrial uses in the cities. The dams are big giants used for our protection in flood control and supply us with a steady flow of water to meet our needs.

In 1992 what is happening to the Colorado River area

around Bullhead City would indeed shock the early pioneers. They could never in their wildest dreams imagine a huge gambling resort area which now occupies the Nevada side of the river. It is the city of Laughlin, Nevada, that now has about fifteen gambling casinos. Bullhead City is on the Arizona side and since gambling is still not legal in Arizona, the people in the state of Arizona flock to the area in great numbers. Along with the Arizonians are thousands of Californians and others who are gradually making the spot another Las Vegas. People take advantage on the Arizona side of the free ferry ride to the Laughlin side. Laughlin is about thirty-five miles from Kingman, Arizona.

Bullhead City has become the mobile home capital of Arizona. This is a popular way to take up residence in the gambling area. Many have a second home in this fashion while living in other homesites in California or Arizona.

Chapter Fourteen

INDIANS IN ARIZONA

I have no knowledge of a case on record where a white man has been convicted and punished for defrauding an Indian. Greed and avarice on the part of the whites . . . In other words, the almighty dollar is at the bottom of nine tenths of all our Indian trouble.

General Crook, Indian fighter
Gila country, 1886

Today there is a great interest in Indian culture in this country. Television and various courses in our schools have done much to explain to the American public the interesting history and culture of the American Indian. Indian folklore is not dead and its artifacts are not antiques. On the contrary, the Indian culture in Arizona is a vital contributing force; it is a vital phenomenon of human experience existing in the midst of the dominant society.

Arizona has more Indians than any other state in the Union. Historically, Indian culture has always had to cope with its natural environment through adaptive processes that resulted in harmonies with nature, rather than processes which led to the control and change of natural environment. The Indian has been

139

able to do this in Arizona.

Let us look at some of the notable tribes of Indians that number more than 200,000 in the state of Arizona.

THE HOPI

The Hopi live in compact villages, called pueblos, on three mesas roughly seventy-five miles northeast of Flagstaff. Their ancestors had lived in northeastern Arizona for over two thousand years before they settled permanently on the mesas over six hundred years ago. The Hopi are well known for their craft work, particularly their carved and colorful painted wooden Kachina dolls, their fine pottery, their coiled and wicker basketry, and in recent years their overlay silver jewelry.

THE NAVAJO

The largest tribe living on the largest reservation in the United States, the Navajo are rapidly increasing in number and quickly adopting the white man's way of life. They are semi-nomadic, moving with their sheep and goats from winter to summer homes and doing some farming.

The Navajo are famous as weavers and silversmiths. The possession and display of jewelry is a significant measure of the individual's wealth; consequently quantities of "hard goods" may deck the satin skirts and velvet blouses of the women or the store-bought shirts and jeans of the men.

THE APACHE

Living on the San Carlos and White Mountain Reservations, the Apache are known as the Indian cattlemen. The men dress in typical cowboy outfits, while the women prefer long, full-tiered skirts with loose over-blouses patterned after the late nineteenth-century dresses. The Apache still excel at basket making.

The Apache of Arizona call themselves "inde" or "tinde"

meaning "the people". Until they were subdued, they were the most warlike tribe in the Southwest. Their fighting spirit was especially evident in the period from 1870 to 1900, when the encroachments of white settlers aroused them to fierce resentment. Probably the most famous of these uprisings was the series of raids waged by Geronimo.

Geronimo was born in southern Arizona in 1829 and his Apache name was Go Khla Yeh. When Mexican soldiers attacked one of the Apache camps and killed his mother, wife, and three children, Geronimo went on the warpath. Between 1881 and 1886, he led several outbreaks, killing and plundering as he made his way into the mountains of Arizona and Mexico. He was eventually captured and sent to reservations in Florida, Alabama, and Oklahoma. He became a star attraction at the world's fair in St. Louis, Missouri, and in Buffalo, New York. He joined the Dutch Reformed Church at Fort Sill, Oklahoma, in 1903, but was expelled for gambling.

In 1905, Geronimo rode in the inaugural parade of President Theodore Roosevelt. Later he visited the President with five other Indian chiefs.

He died at Fort Sill on February 17, 1909.

PIMA and PAPAGO

Similar in cultures, the Pima (river dwellers) and Papago (bean people) dress in modern western styles. Most of them have become Christianized. Learning to farm with heavy machinery and large-scale agricultural planning, they are developing their economy on long range programs. The Papago also raise cattle and have fine herds. The Pima and Papago make baskets, weaving them with willow and yucca fibers.

THE PAIUTE

Living in the far northwestern part of Arizona and on reservations in four other states—California, Nevada, Utah, and

Oregon—most Paiutes speak English, live and dress like the white man, and engage in cattle raising and wage work as their major source of income. The most distinctive craft created by the Paiute is the wedding basket, a coiled, shallow basket used by the Navajo Indians because of its finish and symbolic design.

THE CHEMEHUEVI

The Chemehuevi Indians are located on the Colorado River Reservation. Deserving of mention, although no longer produced, are the famous small, coiled baskets for which the Chemehuevi are well known. The baskets are simple bowls or jars with patterns usually worked in black or an occasional dark red.

THE COCOPAH

The Cocopah tribe lives on the lower Colorado. The majority of the tribe work on the farms of white men. They were noted for their skills in piloting steamboats up and down the Colorado. Today they number only a few hundred.

THE MOHAVE

The majority of the Mohave live on two reservations— the Fort Mohave and the Colorado River Reservations. Most of their crafts are dying out, and the Mohave women have turned from making pottery to the creation of ties, belts, capes, and purses made from glass beads.

THE HAVASUPAI

The beautiful Havasu Canyon is the reservation home of the Havasupai Indians. Relatively isolated, these people sustain themselves with farming and off-reservation wage work. Most of their native crafts are gone except for the conical burden baskets which the women still make.

THE HUALAPAI (or WALAPAI)
Neighbors of the Havasupai, the Hualapai live in and above the canyons leading down to the Colorado River and are primarily cattlemen and lumbermen. Their basketry is well made and follows traditional designs.

THE YAVAPAI
Nomadic in nature, the Yavapai have separated into different groups, some living with Apache bands, and others at the Ft. McDowell Reservation, the Camp Verde Reservation, and the Yavapai Reservation. The Yavapai may be said to be farmers, wage workers, industrial employees, or cattle raisers, depending upon the reservation on which they live. The only native craft that survives is basketry.

THE MARICOPA
Spread between the Gila River and Salt River Reservations, the Maricopa have adopted the Pima economy and have borrowed many of the Pima crafts. Maricopa potters create unusual-shaped ceramic bowls, many of which have an admirable high polish and all of which have been popular commercially.

THE YUMA
Some of the Yuma Indians live in California, but many of them work in Arizona making their living by wage work. Their crafts are disappearing and only a little pottery is still made.

Arizona is Indian country. Its twenty-one reservations cover nearly twenty million acres or approximately twenty-seven percent of the state. The several reservations' geography and climate range from the cool high plateau country of the Hopi and Navajo to the low arid Sonoran Desert lands of the Cocopah and Papago.

Natural resources on the reservations include coal, natural gas, copper, gemstones, sand and gravel, stone, asbestos, volcanic cinder, agricultural and grazing lands, and timber.

Scenic and recreational resources include national monuments, such as the beautiful Canyon de Chelly on the Navajo Reservation, Pipe Springs on the Kaibab Paiute Reservation, and many ancient ruins of Indian cultures of the distant past. Further examples include water sports on the Colorado River Reservation; hunting, fishing, and skiing at Sunrise Park on the Fort Apache Reservation; the Grand Canyon on the Hualapai Reservation; Kitt Peak Observatory and the historic San Xavier Mission on the Papago Reservation; and Salt River Canyon and San Carlos Lake on the San Carlos Reservation. But the Indian people and their rich culture and crafts are the reservations' greatest attraction.

The lofty mesa-top-pueblo villages of the Hopi and the remote and beautiful canyon home of the Havasupai draw many visitors. Indian craftsmen fashion the exquisite Navajo silver and turquoise jewelry, Pima and Papago basketry and Hopi pottery and hand-carved Kachina dolls.

The appeal of the Indian reservations is not limited to the tourist and outdoor recreation seeker. Business and industry have discovered the advantages of locating on the reservations.

Property tax advantages are available to businesses locating on the reservation lands. Government agencies such as the Economic Development Administration, Farmers Home Administration, Small Business Administration, Four Corners Regional Commission, and Bureau of Indian Affairs are prepared to provide to businesses a variety of services and assistance ranging from information to loans, grants, and training programs.

Several reservations including the Colorado River, Gila

River, Hopi, Navajo, Papago, Salt River, and San Carlos have developed industrial parks with complete utilities, transportation facilities, and a ready labor force. Leases are available at competitive terms.

New business and industry ventures include electronics, retail trade and services, a wide range of light manufacturing, recreational and tourism facilities, agriculture and related processing, mining and utilities to name a few.

The State of Arizona does not tax Indian lands and Indian-owned property on reservations. Incomes of Indians residing on reservations are also not taxed if wholly derived from reservation sources. Indian people of Arizona are exempt from state and local sales taxes on consumer goods purchased on the reservation, unless such taxes are imposed by the tribal government. Arizona does tax the property and business transactions of non-Indians who operate on reservations and Indians who live or work off reservations.

In 1986 two Indian women entered the Arizona Women's Hall of Fame. Elected for their service and contributions to the State of Arizona, the new inductees bring to 34 the number so honored since the Hall of Fame was established in 1981 by the Arizona Women's Commission. The women are:

Viola Jimulla (1878-1906), a Yavapai tribal chieftain, who helped establish the reservation near Prescott.

Nampeyo (1860-1942) a Hopi potter and archaeologist known in the Indian art world as "the Old Lady," and credited with reviving the art of fine pottery making.

Almost all Indian tribes in Arizona now have gambling as a legal entity on their reservations. The prosperous casinos are popular recreational centers. The lucrative profits from many gambling casinos enhance the educational and social life of the Indian tribes.

The Fort McDowell Casino is one of the largest Indian gambling centers in Arizona. At the present time the gross revenue is about a million dollars a day. The tribe is now building a 35 million dollar golf course not far from the casino.

Chapter Fifteen

BISBEE DEPORTATION

The main reason why there is so much crime among our young people in Arizona and in our country is because most mothers are working. They are not at home to take care of the children. There is no substitute for mothers.
Barry Goldwater
Interview with author, January 1994

On June 26, 1917, a strike was called in Bisbee, Arizona, probably the most famous strike in all of Arizona history. Around two thousand miners walked off their jobs at three copper companies which were in operation at that time: the Copper Queen Division of Phelps Dodge Corporation, the Calumet and Arizona Mining Company and the Shattuck Arizona Mining Company.

Two labor unions were involved. One was the International Union of Mine, Mill and Smelter Workers and the other was the International Workers of the World's Metal, Mine Workers Industrial Union, better known as the Wobblies. The latter was usually allied to Communist ideology and it had a reputation at that time for agitating against capitalistic enterprises. The Wobblies brought on the strike and had some help from the other union. At that time unions were not too particular as to what methods were used to obtain some of their objectives, and the Wobblies in particular had become Public Enemy Number One in the minds of most people.

Because of the war, there was a great demand for copper and Bisbee had attracted a number of workers who were not ideal citizens. There was the usual aura of suspicion about events and people that always seems to abound during perilous times in our history.

Out of nowhere a special task force was organized called the Workmen's Loyalty League. These were the good guys who decided that enough was enough. They numbered about two thousand and they were well organized. Their enemies were the strikers and the Wobblies in particular.

On July 12, 1917, starting early in the morning, Bisbee started a roundup of the strikers in a fashion unprecedented in our nation's history. The deputized Loyalty League, in Army style form, rounded up about 1,186 bad guys from all parts of Bisbee. They were placed in cattle cars by force and their destination was to be New Mexico.

To make sure that federal and state authorities would not interfere, all telegraph and telephone communications were cut off.

The train left in the afternoon on that memorable day of July 12, 1917, in what was to be called in history the "Wobbly Special." Riding on top of the cars were about two hundred heavily armed guards, all members of the Loyalty League.

This notorious train was to arrive that same day in Columbus, New Mexico, at nearly midnight. In Columbus there was a problem. Officials at that city refused to allow the prisoners to disembark. In desperation the train moved about 15 miles toward the Arizona border to a little village in New Mexico called Hermanas. There the prisoners were told to scatter to the four winds and were warned never to enter Bisbee because the threat of death would hang over them. A U.S. Army cavalry unit was to arrive some hours later to escort the men to a tent stockade where they were given provisions and some protection against the heat of the day. The Army did not consider the men to be prisoners and, of course, they were allowed to go free. Apparently the Army took good care of the men, for not until September did the last group leave and only after the Army began a program of giving them half rations.

This whole incident was to be called in the annals of Arizona history the Bisbee Deportation. It was to eventually obtain worldwide publicity and many wondered about justice in the Wild West.

The Wobblies actually increased their memberships throughout the U.S. because of what happened in Bisbee. President Wilson created a special commission to be sent to Bisbee to investigate the whole matter. One of the members of the commission was Felix Frankfurter who was to later become a justice of the Supreme Court. The Arizona governor at that time, Thomas E. Campbell, and his state attorney, Wiley E. Jones, personally investigated.

The Wobblies continued to agitate at mining camps other than Bisbee. The latter incident seemed to spur them on to greater organization. It must be reported that they were similarly deported in smaller numbers from Jerome and from Globe. However, these incidents were to never gain the notoriety of the famous Bisbee Deportation.

To this day there are divisions of thought as to whether the Bisbee Deportation was right or wrong. One thing is certain, Bisbee was put on the map and receives national attention to this day over the famous strike.

It is to be noted that the Bisbee Deportation incident was directed by Cochise County Sheriff Harry Wheeler. But he was a mere pawn in the political and economic copper dynasties run by copper barons and politicians who profited handsomely from the mine revenues. Phelps Dodge orchestrated the whole affair and even distributed guns and ammunition to the posse. In the long drawn out affair between management and labor, the former was helped to a great degree by the special friendship that existed between President Woodrow Wilson and Cleveland H. Dodge, a director of Phelps Dodge. Also in the governor's race of 1916, Thomas Campbell, a Republican and very pro-management, defeated George W.P. Hunt, whose platform favored unions. Then there was the news media at that time that whipped up sentiment against the unions.

Absentee owned mines prospered at Bisbee, Jerome, Globe-Miami and at Clifton-Morenci. Mexican workers were paid half of what others earned. Walter Douglas , who became President of the American Mining Congress, drew other owners to help in the fight to ruin the unions. History can ask this question at the time: Was the deck stacked against the miners and their unions?

Chapter Sixteen

THE FAMOUS YUMA CROSSING

Distance often gives erroneous interpretation, as well as en-
chantment. We think that this is somewhat the case with Yuma.
It is not an Indian village; though an Indian village exists con-
tiguous to it, and a full representation of the old Yuma tribes
constitute an equal half of its daily population. Blanketed and
half nude Indians associate as intimately with the white (what
few there are here) as do the Mexicans themselves. The town
itself is strictly of Mexican origin, and savors of all the loose-
ness and primitiveness characteristic of the smaller, out of the
way towns in the Republic of Mexico. One sees a mass of one
story buildings, built of adobe, and roofed with mud. Some white-
washed and with a clear appearance; while others as embodi-
ment of the filth of the area.

> E. Conklin
> In *Picturesque Arizona*, 1878

Of all the cities and areas in the United States, very few
have played such a powerful role in history as the Yuma Crossing. Not only is Yuma, Arizona, one of our oldest cities, but it
has had a very historical impact on the history of the Southwest. It was the meeting place of the Gila and Colorado Rivers.

All movement going into southern California and, for that matter, the whole of the Southwest, went through Yuma and its famous crossing.

In 1826 Lt. R.W.H. Hardy, of the British Navy, traveling in Mexico, chartered the 25-ton schooner Bruja (Sea Witch) in Guaymas, Mexico, and came to the Yuma Crossing.

In 1827 Sylvester and James Ohio Pattie, two fur trappers, visited Yuma and went south to the Gulf of California. James Ohio Pattie's *Personal Narrative* remains to this day as a wonderful little book concerning the story of early trade in the Southwest. During 1825 and 1826, the Patties trapped on the Gila and operated copper mines at Santa Rita. The younger Pattie discovered a route from New Mexico to the eastern boundary of California. He explored much of the Colorado River (including the Grand Canyon), traversed the Central Rocky Mountain region as far north as the Yellowstone and the Platte, and followed the Arkansas to the south, where he crossed to the Rio Grande which brought him to Santa Fe, New Mexico. At one time, while in California with a vaccine which his father had discovered, he helped vaccinate about 22,000 persons against a ravaging epidemic of smallpox. In the words of Reuben Gold Thwaites, "brave, honest, God-fearing, vigorous in mind and body, dependent on their own resources, the Patties belonged to that class of Americans who conquered the wilderness and pushed the frontier westward."

With the advent of the war with Mexico in 1846, the Yuma Crossing, still under the flag of Mexico, had tremendous strategic importance.

There were two objectives in the overall policy of President Polk. One was to win the northern provinces of Mexico. On the day war was declared against Mexico, he told the cabinet: "In making peace with our adversary, we shall acquire California, New Mexico, and other further territory, as an indemnity for this war, if we can." The second objective was to end the struggle quickly.

In keeping with this plan, the "Army of the West" was formed with the aim of winning California and New Mexico. Col. Stephen W. Kearny assembled this force at Ft. Leavenworth on the Missouri River in the spring of 1846. He recruited three hundred regular dragoons, a thousand Missouri frontiersmen, five hundred Mormon youths who volunteered from the camp at Council Bluffs, Iowa, where Brigham Young was preparing to lead his people westward, and enough miscellaneous recruits to bring the total to 2,700 men.

While in Santa Fe, New Mexico, Kearny eventually divided his army into three parts and each had a mission. One of these armies numbering about three hundred men, along with the colonel, started for California and passed through Yuma. Along the way, they met Kit Carson, bearing the welcome news that California was already won.

Kearny then sent a large segment of his army back to Santa Fe. He enlisted the aid of Carson to help him trek the remaining miles to California with about one hundred men.

Following Kearny across the plains came the so-called Mormon Battalion, which had enlisted in the U.S. Army for one year. This energetic group was under the command of Philip St. George Cooke. They did not take the same route as Kearny's battalion, rather they passed through Yuma several months behind him. The long 1,400 mile wagon route taken by Lt. Col. Cooke and his men was to become famous over the years. As Cooke wrote in his report, "Marching half naked and half fed, and living upon wild animals, we have discovered and made a road of great value to our country. History may be searched in vain for an equal march of infantry." They arrived in San Diego in January, 1847.

For many years, the Indians in the Yuma area had a profitable business of helping people across the wild Colorado. With the discovery of gold in California, the increase in passengers made it necessary for a ferry service to operate and Lt. Cave J. Coutts was the first ferry master. He operated the ferry in the late fall of 1849. He was a soldier in command of an escort attached to the boundary surveyor team. On the first of November, 1849, a flatboat, which had made the voyage down the Gila from the Pima villages with a Mr. Howard and family and two men, arrived at the surveyor's camp. The lieutenant immediately purchased the flatboat and used it as a ferry during the remainder of his stay. This was the beginning of the ferry business in the Yuma area.

The year 1849 was a memorable one in the history of the Yuma Crossing. Thousands of gold seekers heading for the rich lodes in California passed through this area. Some historians claimed that as many as 60,000 miners or prospectors went through the Yuma Crossing in a 12-month period.

With the end of the war with Mexico in 1848, and the signing of the Treaty of Guadalupe Hidalgo, many problems faced the government in Washington. One was the fact that many areas in the new lands of New Mexico and California did not have proper markings or any accurate maps. Thus, the U.S. Government sent several survey teams into this new territory, many of which passed through Yuma.

One of the first survey teams came in 1851, led by Capt. Lorenzo Sitgreaves with a party of infantrymen. He crossed the area of the 35th parallel and made a careful examination of the land which some years later became the route of the Santa Fe Railroad.

In 1853 Lt. Amiel Whipple, a veteran of the Boundary Survey, came into the Yuma area with a group of topographical engineers.

While Whipple was locating passengers to the San Francisco Mountains, another expedition, under Lt. John G. Parke, arrived in Yuma for topographical study.

The majority of the early writings about the vicinity at

the junction of the rivers indicate that there were three settle-ments on the Arizona side of the Colorado River, all within a distance of a mile or so. One of these became known as Colo-rado City and consisted of only one adobe building that was used as a customs' house. A short distance away was another small settlement called Arizona City, which had half a dozen adobe buildings, including two stores, two saloons, and a post office. The third settlement was located at the ferry one mile below the junction. Here were found two stores, two blacksmith shops, a hotel, several houses, and a stage station.

Within the seven years between 1854 and 1861, the three settlements evolved into what is Yuma today, although it was not designated officially as such until a bill was passed by the 7th Arizona Legislature in January, 1873, changing the name from Arizona City to Yuma.

The town site that had been laid out by the Poston Party in 1854 was duly registered in the records of San Diego County. For some time, Yumans paid their taxes to the tax collector from San Diego.

The first mail route from the Pacific coast was the same one which had been used by the herdsmen. Mail eastbound from California started from San Diego in October, 1857. Stages were not used until supply depots had been established along the road. Before this was done, the mail was carried in saddle bags. To take the letters east from Yuma to Tucson required three days and two nights in a buckboard. Horses were changed every 15 miles, and as a rule there was at least one passenger. The great-est Apache danger came in the stretch of desert between Oatman Flats 90 miles east of Yuma, and Picacho Hill near Tucson. The following was taken from the San Diego *Herald* for November 21, 1857, describing the stage route from that city east:

> Stage fares from San Diego are as follows: To Yuma, $35.00; to Tucson, $75.00; to El Paso,

$120.00; to San Antonio, $150.00 including meals. Each man proposing to go should provide himself with a rifle and 100 cartridges; a Colt's revolver and two pounds of balls, knife, and a sheathe; a pair of thick boots and woolen pants . . . a soldier's overcoat . . . such money as he takes should be in silver and small gold.

In September, 1858, John Butterfield from New York signed a six-year contract to carry the mail through from St. Louis to San Francisco, twice weekly, at $600,000 a year. The Butterfield Line which afterward became the Overland Mail Company represented the height in stagecoach efficiency. It had 100 Concord coaches, 1,000 horses, 500 mules and 750 employees, and it operated between San Francisco and Tipton, Missouri, at the western end of the Missouri Pacific Railroad. The contract with the government required the line to make the 2,759 mile trip in 25 days; but the usual time was 23, and once, it was cut down to 16 days. Although it provided the best service possible, the Butterfield was noted for more speed than comfort. The heavy Concord coaches were drawn by teams of four broncos, which were changed at stations scattered along the route. There was an exciting interval of bucking and stampeding when a fresh team was harnessed, and throughout the journey the coach often lurched dangerously on and off the road.

Eventually, the Civil War disrupted means of communication in the Southwest and transportation in Arizona suffered a setback from which it was long in recovering. Some of the stock and other property of the Butterfield Line was confiscated by the Confederates in Texas in 1861, and the lack of military protection in Arizona against the Indians and road agents was an added reason for discounting the service. During the 1860s and early 1970s, there were a few stagecoach and horseback mail lines operating in Arizona. And there were steamboats on the Colorado River, but in the main, Arizona was virtually cut off from adequate communication with the outside world. There was little intercourse even between points within the territory during this period.

The years 1858 and 1859 were important years in the Yuma area. They brought permanent residents, a new steamer, and the discovery of gold on the Gila.

Many Americans and Mexicans who returned from California were frustrated because they did not find gold, and they stopped along the areas of the Yuma Crossing and hunted for the rich, yellow lode.

Jacob Snively, a man from Texas, found the dust about eighteen miles above Fort Yuma. News spread all over the United States and, for a while, the Yuma area was a repetition of the California gold strike. The area where gold was found by Snively became Gila City, and about a thousand people suddenly appeared to make the city a new hub of activity. The gold rush was on. The *San Francisco Chronicle* in 1854 had this to report:

It appears from what I can learn that these mines are situated on the Gila, about eighteen miles from Fort Yuma, on the north bank, northwest from Yuma itself. By the river, it is about forty miles from the diggin's. There is a flat bottom or overflowed sand intervening between the river and the mountains, and the gold is found in the gulches and canyons leading down from the mountains into the Gila. The workmen here and all around are busily engaged in making tools and other appliances used for mining purposes. One wagon load of implements has already departed and it is supposed the miners have been supplied with the necessary instruments—such as picks, shovels, rockers, etc. The climate and temperature is represented to be similar to that of the hottest parts of California. Mr. White who owns a ranch on the Gila, some fifty miles above Fort Yuma, states that there are eleven immigrant families living there at present and some forty or fifty miners at work; and those who worked steadily were averaging over five dollars a day. He further stated that Mr. Riddle had worked in the mines one month and had taken out five hundred dollars of ore. Mr. Birch, who has been working there two months, has taken out eight hundred dollars. Mr. Johnson, who has worked nearly a month, has taken out $250. The dirt after being dug out of the face of the hills and in the gulches is packed and shipped to the river, and washed, which renders mining a very laborious experience and tedious way of getting rich. As to the extent of the diggin's, Mr. White estimates that they extend sixteen miles up and down, on both sides of the river.

However, the gold strike did not last long. There was no rich discovery of any kind. The settlement soon vanished and Gila City became a ghost town.

In 1862 Arizona City suffered a severe flood. At this time the Gila River overflowed her banks to such an extent, that water stood twenty feet deep on a ranch in the bottom lands just above the town. The town virtually had to be rebuilt again. This was one of many disasters that the future area of Yuma was to suffer.

In 1863 Mineral City was founded. The year is also important because the Castle Dome mines were discovered and Arizona became a Territory.

In 1864 Yuma County was laid out with La Paz as the

county seat and it was in this year that the first Pony Express came to Yuma. But in 1867, Yuma, as we know it, began to mature as a site. Permanent homes replaced huts; there were streets and new stores. Mexicans came from Sonora and many came from California. The rich soil near the river produced abundant crops. Wagon factories were established to take care of the overland freighters.

In 1866 the post office was established and the Arizona Vigilantes organized.

In 1870, Arizona City was made the county seat of Yuma County. When the San Diego tax collector arrived in the following fall, there was trouble. When he demanded that the taxes be paid in gold coin, an excited citizen swore out a warrant charging the man with an attempt to collect money under false pretenses. Fortunately for him, some of the more calm citizens deposited bail for his temporary release to appear in court.

Immediately the troubled man wrote to San Diego to inquire what action he should take. His friends advised him to leave the place under cover of darkness. No time was lost in doing this, and his bondsmen were left in a bad state of mind. All of them declared they would never pay another cent to the San Diego authorities, and from that time on the citizens of Yuma have carried out their threat. History seems to record the fact that the people of Yuma always wanted to be identified with the area known as Arizona.

Political organization followed on the heels of settlement in the West. After the admission of Kansas as a state in 1861, the remaining territories of Washington, New Mexico, Utah, and Nebraska were divided into smaller and more convenient units. By the close of the sixties territorial governments were in operation in the new provinces of Nevada, Colorado, Dakota, Arizona, Idaho, Montana, and Wyoming. The political map of the United States was complete except for the division of the Dakotas and the organization of the Indian Territory, the future

Oklahoma.

Shortly after the gold and silver seekers had built a mineral empire, another great economic province began to take shape in the last frontier. The cattle kingdom was born on the Great Plains, its imperial boundaries stretching from the plains of Kansas to California and from Texas to Canada. Like the mining domain, it had a brief and brilliant existence, from approximately 1865 to 1885, and during the period, it influenced materially the course of national development, and added another colorful chapter to the record of the area now known as Arizona and California.

The rise of the cattle kingdom was directly related to the expanding industrial society of urban America. The multitude of new metropolitan centers created a new, huge market for meat and other foods, and this was particularly true of California. Hence, the business of herding cattle from Texas to California by way of Yuma came into existence.

This venture of herding animals all the way from the Rio Grande region to the markets on the Pacific Coast started about 1847. The route followed was the famous old trail from the East which crossed the Rio Grande River near El Paso. It traversed the southern edge of both New Mexico and Arizona in a general westerly course, until reaching the boundary between them, some two hundred miles, and thence in the same general direction several hundred miles to Tucson. The trail turned north here for about ninety miles to the Pima Indian villages on the Gila River, then down the southern side of this stream to the Colorado River at Yuma. Thus, thousands of cattle and many cowboys came to the Yuma Crossing.

Cattlemen took the trail to California for the profits were exceedingly large after the Mexican War. The business for ferrying cattle across the water at the junction became so profitable that several concerns entered the field. If the cattlemen were fortunate enough to arrive when the water happened to be at a low stage, the animals waded or swam to the other bank. This would result in quite a saving.

Various factors enabled the cattle industry to spread over the West—the suppression of the Indians, the elimination of the buffalo, the laxity of the land laws—but the most important were the open range and railroads. The open range afforded a huge area for the herds to move about unrestricted. The railroads gave the cattle kingdom access to markets and thus brought it into being. In ancestry, however, the cattle industry was Mexican and Texan. Long before the Americans came to the Yuma Crossing, Mexican ranchers and vaqueros had developed the techniques and tools employed later by the cattlemen and cowboys of the West.

Slowly but surely, Arizona City (Yuma) began to grow. One of the most important families to arrive was the Contreras family. Before Mrs. Contreras died, she had brought twenty-one children into the world.

Francisco Contreras and wife, Delores, went to California from Sonora, Mexico, in 1833. After living in that state for twenty-five years, they came back to the junction of the Gila and Colorado for farming and to prospect for gold. At the time of their arrival, the family consisted of eight or nine children in addition to mother and father. They settled about ten miles north of Fort Yuma on the west bank of the Colorado and called the place El Colorado. The site happened to be near the ruins of San Dionisio Mission which had been destroyed a few years after the middle of the eighteenth century.

A few days after the settlement had been made, one son, Antonio, returned to Los Angeles to induce a former friend to come back with him to establish a general merchandise store. The other members of the family started to prospect for gold. And gold they did find.

Eventually the family opened a general merchandise store and settled in Laguna, a new mining site, to sell their supplies to the many gold seekers coming from Altar, Sonora, Los Angeles, and San Bernardino.

The gold excitement began to subside in about six years. By that time many people had started to farm and raise cattle on both sides of the Colorado. This was the period when the Contreras family moved from Laguna and Colorado Camp to the town site of Yuma which was soon a flourishing village. At first only temporary huts of sticks and mud were erected, but within the ensuing year all the residents began to construct adobe houses. This all took place in 1867, after the territorial government had made a survey of the Yuma site.

In 1864, the United States government established Yuma Depot. The buildings erected were good, substantial structures, and within two weeks after completion, were filled with provisions, camp equipment, and military stores of every description.

The commissary building, two hundred feet in length, fronted on the river, had a track run through the center of the structure. The supplies were unloaded from the steamboats onto cars and hauled either to storerooms, or right through the commissary building to the south end, where from a high platform they were put aboard the immense freight wagons which were in waiting.

The Yuma Depot was the supply station for southern Utah and Nevada, Arizona, New Mexico, and western Texas. The freight was transported from here by wagons which required from sixteen to twenty miles to haul them. Armed escorts accompanied the freight trains to protect them against the bloodthirsty and thieving Apache, but very often, in spite of all care and strategy, the red-handed savage would succeed in overpowering the freighters, killing all they could, robbing the wagons and taking the horses and mules. The old wagon and stage roads through Arizona were the scenes of many a terrible and bloody struggle between the government freighters and the murderous

Apache, whose hand was always ready to rob and kill.

Major William B. Hooper was the first quartermaster in charge of Yuma Depot. He afterwards founded the great mercantile house of Hooper and Company, which firm was eventually succeeded by James M. Barney and Company. Major Hooper is spoken of yet by "old-timers" here as a true, generous, conscientious officer and gentleman.

Three years after being built, Yuma Depot was destroyed by fire and government loss was said to exceed the sum of five hundred thousand dollars. A court of inquiry was convened, and it was found that the fire was caused by some of the boys smoking cigarettes. Captain George W. Hughes was the officer in charge at the time of the conflagration.

The fire took place during the great flood of 1867, and the U.S. wagon master Tom Hayes, who was dispatched to send a telegram to San Diego, had to swim several sloughs with his horse before he reached the telegraph office. The town of Yuma at that time was not blessed with telegraph service.

Within a few weeks after the fire, a large force of carpenters and masons were put to work, and Yuma Depot was rebuilt in "finer style" than ever. During the years following, several officers of the Army, who since have become quite noted, were in command of the depot. Among this number may be named Generals A.G. Rockwell, A.B.D. Lee, and C.E. Dandy. The last officer in charge was Col. Strang who succeeded Maj. J.H. Lord. The government finally abandoned the place in 1880, removing the fine pump, tools, machinery, and supplies to Fort Lowell.

A few of the buildings are now temporarily occupied by persons whose homes were washed away in the late flood.

The steady swish of the red waters of the swift-flowing Colorado are still heard about the old place; the same bright skies are above, but one stir, excitement and hum of the business has been stilled apparently forever, and Old Yuma seems to be sleeping the sleep of eternity.

In 1870, the county seat moved to Arizona City (Yuma). All county files and office equipment were floated down the Colorado River by boat. During this year the first bank also was established.

In 1875, Yuma had developed into a settled community. No longer was it just a place in which to rest before continuing on a journey. Many of the former travelers returned to settle here.

Yuma experienced a progressive growth from 1900 to the era of the First World War. More people began to come into the city and surrounding territory as soon as the Yuma Reclamation Project became a reality. After years of fighting the water question, it appeared that some of the answers to a better distribution of water had been found. People with surplus funds were encouraged to invest their money in irrigation enterprises when water from the Colorado and Gila Rivers became obtainable at reasonable rates.

In January 1910, a Los Angeles architect by the name of R.B. Young was chosen to supervise the construction of the new courthouse and jail. A great deal of wrangling and politics had preceded the final decision in the construction of the county courthouse. Many Yumans wanted it built on Prison Hill. Finally, two contractors, John Wadin and Charles Olcester, started and completed the long delayed courthouse and jail.

The authorities ran into less trouble when they built several new schoolhouses. Before 1908 there was a grammar school on Main Street, and during this year one was built on Second Avenue at a cost of $45,000. The cost of operating these institutions at the time was about $25,000 a year. The major part of the expenditures was used to pay teachers salaries, which ranged from seventy-five to ninety dollars a month.

The citizens had enough foresight to purchase a high school site in 1909. During that year the mayor, Mr. J.H.

Shanssey, sold at public auction block number 121 of the city plat to the board of trustees of the Union High School for the sum of $1,000. In 1912, bonds for $60,000 were sold and by the fall of 1914, the new Union High School was ready for occupancy. This building is located on the mesa between Fourth and Fifth Streets and Fifth and Sixth Avenues.

In addition to the structures described above, a new Elks' Hall was built at a cost of $20,000. It, too, is located on the higher ground above the city.

The banks also came in for their share of expansion after 1900. The Yuma National Bank was granted a charter by the comptroller of the currency on December 14, 1909, and was open for business by January of the new year. This bank at first occupied office space which had been used by the Yuma Title Abstract and Trust Company on Second Street. Four months after it opened its door, there was a reorganization, and a month after that the firm consolidated with the Farmers and Merchants Bank under the name of the Yuma National Bank.

At the same time the banking facilities were moved from Second Street to the quarters occupied by the Farmers and Merchants Bank. In 1916 the concern moved to their new home at the corner of Main and Second Street.

The First National Bank also had a healthy growth. It, too, began to expand after the turn of the century until, in 1913, the capital had increased from $50,000 to $100,000. This institution and the Yuma National Bank were important factors in financing the business life not only of the city of Yuma, but of the farming and mining activities in the adjoining territory as well.

A comparison of Yuma as it was in 1872 with the Yuma of 1913 reveals that only about five of the Americans who had lived there at that early date still remained 41 years later. Main Street was the same but only two houses were left in 1913. Gila Street also remained the same as far as location but not one original house, was discernible by that year. Madison Avenue from Second Street to Third coincided with the streets of 1913. On or near Madison Avenue were found nine houses that had been built by 1872, although it was hard to recognize them at the turn of the century. In the section beginning with First Avenue extending toward the west and south, not a single home could be found that had been there in 1872. By 1913 the mesa had become the residential district of the city. Before this date the locality had been the favorite resort for horseback riding and driving, and the site of a race track.

A few years after the first decade of the twentieth century the automobile began to appear in Yuma in ever-increasing numbers. On January 16, 1913, Mr. W.M. Winn received his first carload of Fords direct from the factory. The coming of so many automobiles brought about demands for a new highway bridge across the Colorado River. Consequently, by February the U.S. government had passed a measure matching the Arizona legislature's $25,000 appropriation. It was now up to California to vote a similar amount in order to construct the proposed bridge. Since the lawmakers were slow in obtaining the money, the people in California raised the necessary money through donations.

In April, 1915, the job was completed and a great celebration was undertaken. On the 11th of the month 25 automobiles passed over the new structure on their way to Holtville, California.

The coming of the automobile also created a demand for paved highways. The first large project in Yuma was the Main Street paving job The contract was let to the O. and C. Construction Company in November, 1916, and the work was completed by March, 1917.

Today Yuma has a population of about 60,000 and it has a booming tourist trade. The Mexican free port city of San Luis is located 14 miles southwest of Yuma.

Four highly productive irrigated farming areas totaling nearly 281,885 acres have made Yuma a principal agricultural trade center. A growing livestock industry is capable of feeding some 250,000 cattle in pen operations annually. It has a very visible and gigantic citrus business and its reputation is known worldwide.

Arizona Western College, a two year junior college, is located in Yuma. Opened in 1963, the college is divided into the liberal arts and science programs which enable students to transfer to the upper division of universities. A vocation-technical program is also available, including courses in electronics and data processing. The author was on its very first faculty. On the campus of Arizona Western College is the Northern Arizona University Center. Graduates of AWC can now take their junior and senior classes leading to a degree with Northern Arizona University.

Visitor attractions in and around Yuma include the Old Territorial Prison, Fort Yuma, and sixteenth century Saint Thomas Mission across the river. Fishing, water skiing, and swimming at lakes along the Colorado River are attractive sports to residents and tourists alike.

Chapter Seventeen

Famous People in Arizona History

Take time to work, it is the price of success. Take time to think, it is the source of power. Take time to play, it is the secret of youth. Take time to read, it is the foundation of knowledge. Take time to worship, it is the highway of reverence. Take time for friendship, it is the source of happiness. Take time to love, it is the one sacrament of life.

Sue Jones, historian

Arizona is noted for its famous and interesting men and women who have participated with their energies and talents to make it the great state that it is. Their number is legion. The author is attempting to name only a very few in this book. It would be impossible to name all of them.

Barry Morris Goldwater

If there was ever a politician who made an impact on his state and on the nation, it has to be Barry Goldwater. He is often called the father of the Republican party. A man of amazing political skills, the noted senator from Arizona won the Republican nomination in 1964 for the presidency, but lost to Lyndon Johnson. Barry Goldwater was born in 1909 in Arizona, the son and grandson of pioneer merchants. Barry grew up in the rustic days of early Phoenix. As a young man he worked in his father's department store and took it over when his father died. He was elected to the Phoenix city council. He later managed Howard Pyle's successful election to become the Republican governor of Arizona. His first Senate election was in 1952 when he defeated the popular incumbent Ernest McFarland. As a senator he became the spokesman for his party and his state. When he retired in 1986, he was one of the most honored and celebrated senators in our nation's history. He was "Mr. Republican."

The author interviewed the senator in his home in 1994. He spoke about his long love affair with the state of Arizona and its people. He believed that Phoenix was well on its way to becoming one of the largest cities in the country. He favored gambling for the Indians in this state, but he opposed total gambling like they have in Nevada. He wanted major league baseball to come to Arizona. (IT HAS!) He favored a dental school for Arizona but wondered why it was never given a big push by the legislature. He felt that we could not build a second medical school at Arizona State University for lack of money. He did not favor a major airport to be built between Phoenix and Tucson. The author was impressed with his keen mind at his age, his quick wit, his knowledge of the history of Arizona and his kind and warm hospitality. Like Marco Polo, who told the world about the greatness of China, so Senator Goldwater told the world about the imperial majesty of Arizona. Goldwater died in 1998.

Charles Trumbull Hayden

Charles Hayden was born in Windsor, Connecticut on April 4, 1825, the son of James T. and Mary Hayden, both of whom were of distinguished colonial ancestry. An intelligent youth, he had the advantages of a good education and was teaching school in New Jersey by the time he was eighteen. Later he taught in Indiana and Missouri before the westward rolling wagons captured his interest.

In 1848 he entered the mercantile business, loading a wagon with goods and hauling it to Santa Fe where he marketed them. The following year he loaded fourteen wagons, hitched six yoke of oxen to each and again set out for Santa Fe, intending to set up in business, but a group of Californians, short of everything because of the gold rush of 1849, bought his whole outfit.

After another trip to Missouri he moved to Santa Fe. In 1858, he moved his headquarters to Tucson, where he contracted with the government to furnish supplies to the soldiers in the region. He also did a brisk freight business with the mines, hauling supplies in and ore out.

Hayden's wagons often were attacked by Apaches, but he was, by this time, an experienced Indian fighter. One military report in 1863 noted that Hayden's train had been attacked by Apaches; but the Indians were driven off after eleven of them were killed, including one of their chiefs, Capinggan.

While in Tucson, Hayden was appointed the area's first probate judge, but according to a letter he wrote later in life, his duties were not too taxing. "In the year I occupied the bench," he wrote, "there was no case of death, not a civil case, and only one criminal case before the court."

He added that five hundred Mexicans composed virtually the entire population of Tucson at that time and they settled their disputes in typical frontier fashion, without the aid of the courts.

Among his other traits was a keen desire to expand his business, and it was during a trip to Fort Whipple in 1870 for this purpose that he first saw the Salt River Valley. He found the river too high to ford and climbed a butte near present-day Tempe to get a better view. What he saw was a valley about fifteen miles wide through which flowed the Salt River for about forty miles westward to its junction with the Gila. Jack Swilling had completed the first irrigation ditch of modern times two years before, and already two thousand acres were under cultivation. Hayden was so impressed with what he saw that he returned to Tucson only long enough to collect his goods. Hastening back to the Salt river, he immediately built a store and established a ferry near where the Tempe Bridge is located today. The area became known as Hayden's Ferry.

In 1871, Swilling organized another irrigation company, the Tempe Irrigating Canal Company, and at his suggestion it offered two thousand inches of water, equivalent to seventeen shares in the company, to anyone who would construct a grist mill of approved capacity. Hayden accepted the offer and began construction in 1872. The mill went into operation in 1874, using water from an extension of the Kirkland-McKinney ditch to turn the grinding stones. The mill had a capacity of about two thousand pounds of flour a day.

No storage reservoirs, such as the Salt River Project has today, were in existence in the 1870s, so the farmers were somewhat at the mercy of the river. When it was high, there was enough water to fill all commitments, but when it was low, everyone took a cut, and Hayden was permitted to operate his mill only two days a week because agriculture had first priority on the water.

Although the man who became known as the Father of Tempe lost an 1874 bid for a seat in Congress, most ventures went well for him. Besides the store, the ferry, and the mill, he owned the blacksmith shop, the carpenter shop, and most of the rest of Hayden's Ferry, in addition to two stores in other locales and an interest in ranch property near Prescott. He helped organize several canal companies on the south side of the river, canals which eventually would become part of the Salt River Valley Water Users' Association system along with the Tempe Canal and other north side canals.

Perhaps, because he was too busy organizing canal companies and expanding his business enterprises, or perhaps because he never met the right girl, Hayden waited until 1876, when he was 51 years old, to take a bride. In that year on October 4, he married Miss Sallie Calvert Davis in Nevada City, California, returning with her to Tempe in 1877. This well-educated, strong-willed pioneer apparently had found a perfect match, for his wife was described as a woman of "unusual force of character and strong intellectual endowments."

The Haydens had four children: Carl, who became and remained until 1968 one of the nation's most revered United States senators; Sallie, who became a teacher; Mary, whose two sons continued to operate the flour mill; and Annie, who died in infancy.

In the year 1900, Charles Trumbull Hayden died, preceding his wife by seven years. He will be remembered as the man who always was willing to lend a helping hand, who commanded the respect and trust of all who knew him, and whose sincerity and integrity were never doubted. His monuments are the city of Tempe, which he founded; the life-giving canal system which he helped develop; and Arizona State University, which came into existence as Tempe Normal School, conceived in the mind of Charles Trumbull Hayden, who donated the land on which it was constructed.

Dwight Bancroft Heard

Dwight Heard was born in Boston on May 1, 1869. It was in Chicago in 1886 at the age of seventeen that he began his business career with a wholesale hardware firm. On August 10, 1894, he married Maie Clay Bartlett.

The following year the couple journeyed west to Arizona. While his father's enthusiasm for the untamed lands on the western horizon undoubtedly played a part in Heard's decision to move, of at least equal importance was a troublesome lung. Shortly after arriving in Arizona, he formed the Bartlett-Heard Land and Cattle Company in partnership with his father-in-law and two years later, established an investment and loan business.

The Bartlett-Heard firm purchased 7,500 acres of land south of the Salt River which were planted in grapes, oranges, and grapefruit. Later it was subdivided into homesites, but Heard continued intensive farming of 1,100 acres which he planted with citrus, cotton, alfalfa, grain, and grapes. With such extensive holdings, it is natural that irrigation was a dominant interest, and he was one of the staunchest advocates of federal legislation to permit the government to undertake reclamation projects. As one of the five persons named to the first Water Storage Commission of Maricopa County, he attempted to persuade Congress to pass the needed legislation. President McKinley seemed indifferent, however, and Congress stalled.

With the assassination of President McKinley on September 14, 1901, Theodore Roosevelt became president and the outlook appeared more favorable. Heard was a friend of Teddy Roosevelt, and he now used all his persuasive powers to urge the president to support an enlightened reclamation policy. His arguments and the arguments of others fell on receptive ears. In 1902, while Heard was in Washington, the National Reclamation Act was passed. The foundation was laid for development of the West.

Heard's friendship with the president was to bear further fruit, for Arizona was not the only area seeking an irrigation project. Heard argued, however, that the five conditions necessary for a successful irrigation project were present in Arizona: (1) an excellent watershed, (2) an easily damable canyon, (3) tillable, fertile soil, (4) large reservoir capacity above the dam site, and (5) a climate providing a long growing season. There seems little doubt that Heard played a significant role in securing for Arizona the first project authorized under the National

Reclamation Act.

Finding an acceptable method of repaying the government for construction of Roosevelt Dam proved difficult. Large landowners such as Heard resented proposals which would saddle them with a disproportionate share of the cost, while small landowners and holders of water rights were equally adamant that their portion of the cost be kept to a minimum. The need was plain, however, and despite heated controversy, a compromise plan was finally agreed upon. That decision made, some four thousand landowners formed the Salt River Valley Water Users' Association to finance construction of the dam. The association was incorporated on February 9, 1903.

Heard's achievements at this point in his life were considerable, but he was just getting started. He was to be a major figure in the fight to prevent joint statehood with New Mexico and in the organization of cooperative marketing associations for hay growers, cotton growers, and grain growers.

In 1912 he followed his friend, President Roosevelt, into the Progressive movement and purchased The *Arizona Republic*, so the party would have a public organ in the territory. In 1924 he was the Republican candidate for governor, but was defeated by about eight hundred votes by former Governor Hunt, 38,372 to 37,571.

In addition to furthering the development of an efficient irrigation system, one of Heard's prime concerns was the highway system, and he served as president of the Arizona Good Roads Association. A small sampling of his other affiliations include the Conservation of Natural Resources Congress, the National Irrigation Congress, National Conservation Congress, Roosevelt Council of Boy Scouts of America, American National Livestock Association, U.S. Chamber of Commerce, Phoenix Community Chest, World Cotton Conference, and many others. He was an officer of virtually every organization with which he was associated.

Despite his many business interests, he took an active part in the life of his church, Trinity Episcopal Cathedral, and enjoyed fishing, golfing, and playing tennis. He also found time to promote Arizona through magazine articles such as "Arizona's Irrigation Development for the Earth".

During World War I he was chairman of the Arizona Council of Defense and with his knowledge of agriculture, succeeded in greatly increasing the state's agricultural production. He also was chairman for the War Camp Community Service and in recognition of these activities was appointed a captain in the Officers Reserve Corps, Eight Corps Area.

Both Heard and his wife were greatly interested in prehistoric research, and they left to the people of Arizona a prehistoric community house which they had uncovered two miles east of Phoenix and a museum to house their collection of the art and handicraft of primitive peoples. Both Pueblo Grande and Heard Museum are major assets of modern-day Phoenix.

Dwight Bancroft Heard died on March 14, 1929. He was survived by Mrs. Heard, who lived until 1951, and by their son, Bartlett Bradford Heard, who had been born on December 1, 1898. Bartlett Heard and his family reside in California.

The Arizona Legislature memorialized him after his death, and a *Phoenix Gazette* editorial called him "fearless, positive and forceful—the very essence of constructive action."

Perhaps the most fitting tribute to this man who had a major role in the formation of the Salt River Valley Water Users' Association and construction of Roosevelt Dam was by historian John R. Murdock, who wrote: "In sober truth, Dwight B. Heard ought to be listed among the half dozen great Americans who are responsible for the extensive achievement of conservation and reclamation throughout the West."

Wilson Wesley Dobson

Dobson arrived in the Salt River Valley in 1886 from California and was impressed with what he saw. He knew fertile land when he saw it and crouched down in the hostile desert to touch the soil and let it run through his fingers. He decided he would homestead this quarter section of land, just outside of the small community of Mesa, Arizona.

One of the first things he did was to build himself a shelter which was more of a shack than anything else. Its size was approximately six feet by ten feet. The floor was dirt.

For three years he would live there under the crudest conditions. Days he would spend working for his neighbors, either irrigating their fields or chopping wood. In the evening he worked his own land, clearing away the mesquite and palo verdes and cacti. His neighbors said they could hear his axe late into the night.

But when those three years passed, Dobson had something to show for his labors. His farm was a going concern, so much so that eventually he was able to acquire adjoining properties, bringing his total acreage to 640.

After building a new house, using rocks which he hauled from the Salt River bed as the foundation, he returned to Canada to marry his sweetheart, Emma Argue, and bring her to his adopted country. She would bear him three children, Wilson, Harold, and a girl, Hazel, who died tragically at a young age. After his wife died, he remarried.

As a farmer, he, of course, realized the value of irrigation and canal systems, and it was no wonder that he became active in the affairs of the Utah Canal Company, eventually becoming a director, then president, of that concern.

Dobson was one of the farmers who actually helped in the construction of the Utah Extension and Eureka Canal. In the future, his experiences with the Utah Canal Company would serve him in good stead.

W.W. Dobson was also a member of the Fourth Legislature, serving during the years 1919-1920. But it was a position he did not like very much. He was disdainful of backslapping and horse trading, and did not hold the label "politician" in high regard.

He was a fine, honorable man, and a steady contributor to the Methodist Church, which he helped to establish. He was a member of the church board and school board.

His feats of stamina and endurance are legion. The quarter section he initially cleared was done solely by pick, shovel, and axe. He as an expert axeman, and made every lick count. The story is told that he once had a contract job of cutting wood, for which he was paid by the cord. When his employer came by to see how he was doing, W.W. explained that he wasn't feeling well and hadn't done very much. The man was amazed to find a woodpile half as high as a house.

There was the time that Dr. Moeur of Tempe told W.W. to rest and relax, that he shouldn't drive himself so hard. The prescription was a trip to the mountains. W.W. went willingly enough, but he stayed only half as long as the good doctor recommended, and while there, cut two carloads of cedar posts!

In summer, when the growing season was over in the Valley, he'd go up to his farms in Canada, and supervise the wheat harvest.

He loved to plant things and watch them grow. The canal bank near his house was covered with fig trees. Many a time he would join the rest of his family and relatives in harvesting the figs and peeling and making them ready for preserving. He had hundreds of these trees, and welcomed travelers and picnickers from Phoenix and the surrounding area to pick them.

W.W. had a sweet tooth for honey. Often he would go off with mask and gloves, come back several hours later, and pass out the sweet stuff to whoever was present at his home.

Dobson was active to the end, but unfortunately, as he grew older, he had many sleepless nights. He also had trouble reaching for a word, and this perplexed this vital, dynamic man.

While visiting in Canada with his wife, he attempted to fix the leaking roof of a house he was renting. On the roof, he suffered a stroke which caused him to lose his eyesight. Even that didn't stop him. In his later years, when he had moved to town, he would spend time visiting his sister who lived on Main Street in Mesa, walking there unaided.

Wilson Wesley Dobson died on May 19, 1940. He was one of the last of that rugged breed who wanted something better and would get it by the sweat of his brow.

John P. Orme

"It is given to but few men to render conspicuous and useful service in nation, state and community for 60 years."

That eulogy was given for John P. Orme in an obituary notice November 13, 1936. It was a tribute to a man whose death commanded notice with headlines reading: *Empire Builder of Valley Dies;* and *Community Builder Helped Develop Valley Area.*

Another name was given to him, too, "Uncle John." That's how he was known to his pioneer friends. Instead of "Uncle John," however, it well could have been "Uncle Arizona," since he helped lay the groundwork for Arizona's present water supply and prosperity.

John P. Orme, an Easterner, came to Arizona for his health and entered upon a new career here—the story of many modern Arizonans. Sandwiched in between the words of the above sentence was a multifaceted service to the Valley that lives on today.

A heritage of government service accompanied John Pickney Orme when he entered this world on November 28, 1852, at Montgomery County, Maryland. The son of Charles and Deborah (Pleasants) Orme, he was a direct descendant of Governor Pleasants of Virginia.

Apparently, however, Orme had no early intentions of becoming a statesman. In 1866 he entered Missouri State University at Columbia, studied civil engineering, and was graduated in 1868. As a resident engineer for the Texas and Pacific Railroad in southeastern Texas, he helped construct one of the first railways between Missouri and Texas.

However, the Lone Star State was not to be his home. Orme wandered across much of the West before settling in Arizona. While serving as a civil engineer in Texas and Louisiana he had become a victim of malaria. His attacks of chills and fever sent him in quest of a healthier climate and he left Texas for Colorado. He stayed there briefly before journeying to Los Angeles to work on a pier. This, however, only aggravated his malaria condition and he came to Arizona.

Phoenix, and the forbidding desert country of rocks, mountains, and sparse vegetation with hot days and cool nights might have seemed an unhealthy country for a frail, bespectacled man whose five-foot, seven-inch frame was racked often with attacks of malaria. Nonetheless, Orme thrived here.

His early employment in Arizona, when Phoenix had a population of only one thousand, was as a mule skinner in the Yuma area. For a short time he freighted wheat to Flagstaff, but a shower of Indian arrows on one of his trips convinced him there were safer ways of making a livelihood. He opened a corral in Maricopa, bought forty acres near the present Phoenix County Club site, and soon thereafter obtained eight hundred acres of land in the Cartwright area and became a cattle rancher.

The need of water for his livestock and crops led him to a study of irrigation, and he rapidly became an authority on the subject. His engineering background stood him in good stead when, with his two brothers, Henry and Lin, he built the eighteen mile long Arizona Canal. John also served as superintendent and director of the canal.

Marriage accompanied Orme's early ranching and farming endeavor. He met his wife, Ella Tompkins, in Phoenix where she had been living since leaving Texas at the age of eight. They were married March 8, 1879.

To this union were born four children: Charles Henry, later to have a "Senior" attached to his name; Ora D.; Winifred D., and Clara E. A strong family man, Orme often told his children, "There is no success in the world if your family's not reared properly." Tragedy struck the family with Mrs. Orme's death in 1898, and her loss deeply affected Orme. He turned to a cousin, Kate Lackland, for aid in rearing the children, and he remained single the rest of his life.

Orme apparently filled this void in his life by turning to public service, for the period shortly after his wife's death found him extremely active in community affairs. Having no hobbies, he plunged himself into his work and politics. "His hobby was work; he was a slave driver; he never stayed still himself and he never let anybody else stay still," recalls his son, Charles Henry. "It seemed like he always was on a school board."

The Arizona pioneer became a member of the Salt River Valley Water Users' Association board of governors in 1904 and continued in that capacity until 1909. The following year he became the association's second president, succeeding B.A. Fowler, and served until May, 1918.

An active Democrat, he was on the Maricopa County board of supervisors for nine years, four of which were as board chairman. He also was a member of the Arizona Constitutional Convention in 1911. Historians refer to him as being known for his well-defined plans, an apparent carry-over of his engineering talents to the political field.

A gregarious man, Orme also became active in numerous organizations. He was a member of the Ancient Order of United Workmen and Independent Order of Odd Fellows, both in Phoenix. His Masonic affiliations included Blue Lodge, Chapter, Commandery, and Shrine.

Orme did much to direct Arizona's growth in unheralded capacities. "He was a very persuasive man who worked behind the scenes," points out his son, Charles Henry. "It was he and Joe Kibbey who got warring factions together" in the water disputes of the era.

Despite his intense interest in the serious problems of early Arizona, Orme was a man with a sense of humor. "He was a great joker," recalls Charles Henry Orme. "At the dedication of Theodore Roosevelt Dam in 1911, he and Teddy Roosevelt and Bishop Atwood, a prominent Episcopalian at that time, stayed overnight together in the same room. My father delighted in telling how Bishop Atwood wouldn't let him and Teddy go to bed until they said their prayers. 'You two old sinners won't get any sleep until you say those prayers,' the bishop told them."

Orme's interest in politics just came naturally to him. He was politically oriented and at the age of 71, he stepped into the role of an Arizona lawmaker. Making his legislative debut in 1923, Orme twice was elected to the House of Representatives. His son was to carry on the tradition, becoming an Arizona state senator in 1952 and serving four terms. The son, Charles, was just as respected in legislative circles as was his dad.

Another family interest, concern with good education, rubbed off on Charles. In 1929 he became the founder of the Orme School, 75 miles north of Phoenix. Orme schools enjoys the reputation of being one of the best private schools in the country.

John P. Orme made his name known throughout Arizona as an engineer, rancher, reclamationist, statesman, and educator. He died on November 12, 1936.

Louis Clarence Hill

Louis Hill was the designer and supervisory engineer of the construction of Theodore Roosevelt Dam, Arizona's great water storage facility. This accomplishment alone launched him upon a long, brilliant career in the construction of many more large, successful dams in the West, including the great Hoover Dam.

In the years that followed, Hill never forgot the importance of the Theodore Roosevelt Dam nor his long personal and often frustrating involvement in this massive creation. Before he died on November 6, 1938, at his home in Pasadena, California, he expressed the wish that his ashes be entombed in Theodore Roosevelt Dam. Accordingly, a receptacle containing his ashes was placed in the top of the dam directly below a bronze marker at the south end of the structure. Hill died at age seventy-three.

Son of a jewelry merchant, Hill attended schools in Detroit. Later, he studied at the University of Michigan, where he earned a degree in civil engineering in 1886, and a second degree in electrical engineering four years later.

His early jobs were varied. He began as draftsman for Detroit Pipe & Foundry. This led to work as a leveler and transitman with the Duluth, Redwing & Southern Railway, and to a position of resident engineer for the Great Northern Railroad. Finally he accepted professorships in physics and electrical engineering at the Colorado School of Mines.

A sense of restlessness continue to plague him, a nagging feeling that life held a deeper purpose for him. It brought him to welcome his appointment on June 8, 1903, as an engineer in the U.S. Reclamation Service.

Two months later he came face to face with his purpose in life, although he did not recognize it at the time. He was assigned to the Salt River Valley in central Arizona.

Hill was placed in charge of the Roosevelt project in the

spring of 1904. He remained in this position until March, 1911.

Roosevelt Dam was an engineering challenge from the very first. Yet the initial stone of the huge structure was not set down until September 20, 1906, and the last stone laid on February 6, 1911.

Much of the preliminary work was devoted to the building of access roads, using Indian labor from the White Mountain Apache tribes. Hill lauded the ability of these Apaches as dependable unskilled laborers and often sent them out on the job in unsupervised squads.

It was necessary to erect a cement plant due to the remoteness of the job site. Hill built such a plant. He also built a small lumber mill and provided needed power by constructing a thirteen-mile power canal for generating electricity.

Each step forward was a tribute to Hill and the men who worked for him, for they had no previous projects of this kind to guide their operations. Decisions were made quickly and with conviction. Hill and his men were motivated by one mutual desire, to build Roosevelt Dam and make it a worthy prototype for similar future projects.

In 1911, the 284-foot high structure, from bedrock, was completed with its turbines ready to generate electricity. Roosevelt was the largest dam built to that date in the country, but the cost had reached the frightening amount of $5.4 million.

Jerry Colangelo

In the state of Arizona, which is approaching a population count of about five million, there is one name that is a household word and that name is Jerry Colangelo. He is the greatest "sport mogul" in the history of Arizona. A very wealthy man who came from modest means and an Italian background, he is a self-made man, having no family to bankroll his successful climb from Mr. Average Man to what he is today.

Colangelo's sports empire consists of the following:
Arizona Diamondbacks: managing general partner.
Phoenix Suns: president and chief executive officer.
Phoenix Mercury: chairman of the board.
Arizona Rattlers: chairman of the board.

Honors:
4 NBA Executive of the Year: 1976, 1981, 1989, 1993
3 Most Influential Business Person in the Valley: 1994, 1995, 1996

Clearing hurdles has been a way of life for Colangelo, whose story began in the "Hungry Hill" neighborhood of Chicago Heights, and continued to Bloom Township High School, where as a youth he was one of the top pitchers on a team that also featured the talents of future New York Yankee Jim Bouton. On the hardwood, Colangelo captured All-State honors, leading Bloom Township to a 49-8 mark and two appearances in the Illinois State tournament. His athletic abilities led to 66 college scholarship offers for basketball and seven for professional baseball contracts. He was remembered to the neighborhood with the dedication of the Jerry Colangelo Gymnasium at Bloom Township on November 10, 1996.

He initially selected the University of Kansas, but transferred to the University of Illinois. Unfortunately, a high school arm injury to Colangelo limited his playing career to just two seasons of competitive baseball at Illinois, and his athletic focus turned to hoops. He earned All-Big-Ten honors for the Illini, averaging 15 points a game, served as team captain as a senior and was eventually an inductee into the Illinois Basketball Hall of Fame.

Colangelo's professional career in athletics began with the Chicago Bulls as head scout and director of merchandising in 1966. Just two years later, at the age of 28, he was the youngest general manager in professional sports, taking over the reins of the Phoenix Suns. He held that role until October, 1987, when he led a group of investors that purchased the Suns franchise for $44.5 million, and he has served as the team president and CEO since.

In 1993, the same year he earned an unprecedented fourth NBA Executive of the Year award, Colangelo began assembling yet another group of investors that would eventually convince the expansion committee that big league baseball was not just a spring fling in the Valley.

The assertive and confident style of management that directed the Suns to seven consecutive 50-win seasons, and three appearances in the Western Conference finals, was now headed to another major sport. On behalf of the potential ownership group, he negotiated a deal with the Maricopa County Board of Supervisors that enabled the county to fund $238 million toward the construction of what is now Bank One Ballpark.

Baseball fans throughout the Southwest now have an opportunity to watch Jerry Colangelo operate the Diamondbacks in the same manner that made the Suns one of the most admired franchises in all of sports. He wasted no time applying his trademark of doing business in a first class manner, hiring manager Buck Showalter two years before the actual baseball team would even be assembled.

When one obtains great success in life, he becomes a target for countless critics. Jerry Colangelo has his. In the past ten years, he has negotiated contracts worth a billion dollars. He does it with class and honesty. He has meant a great deal to this Valley. His charity work is monumental. He has been a Marco Polo in telling us all that there is life and rewards for those who work hard and are honest. Downtown Phoenix redevelopment didn't happen without his time, money and zeal. Nobody will deny that he single-handedly has turned Phoenix into a sports mecca. It was not easy.

Harold C. Giss

Extravagant claims are made often in the world of politics but no one will deny that the number one man in the history of modern Yuma was Harold C. Giss. This elder statesman and civic leader supreme dominated the political and civic life of Yuma and Arizona from 1948 until he died in 1973. During that time he was one of the most influential men in legislative circles in this state.

Giss was born in Minneapolis, Minnesota, on February 5, 1906. When he was ten years old, the family left for Los Angeles.

He married Goldie Stool of Del Rio, Texas, and they first arrived in Yuma in 1938. He purchased a department store, the Emporium, and he was its guiding light for many years.

Giss and his wife were blessed with three fine sons, Maurice, Kenneth, and Gerald. Maurice was the Executive Director of the Bicentennial Commission for the State of Arizona in 1976.

Giss entered politics in 1948, when he was first elected to the House of Representatives. In two years, he was elected senator and served with distinction in that capacity until he died.

The esteem in which Senator Giss was held in Yuma was vividly manifested on May 15, 1965. On that day one thousand state, city, and county leaders (including this author) gathered to pay homage to him at a testimonial dinner. The author was greatly impressed by the respect and love displayed by all for this great man.

He was a man who cared for people. Many will testify that he was the best lawmaker in the history of the State of Arizona. He left his mark on Arizona as few have done. People loved Senator Giss.

Dennis Deconcini

Dennis Deconcini was born in Tucson in 1937. He attended public schools in Tucson and Phoenix and received his bachelors and law degrees from the University of Arizona.

In 1959, after a tour of duty in the U.S. Army as a lieutenant, he entered private practice of law with his father, a former justice of the Arizona Supreme Court. He was special counsel to the governor in 1965, and served as Pima County Attorney. A Democrat, he was elected to the U.S. Senate in 1976 and left the Senate in 1994.

General George Crook (1928-1890)

George Crook was recognized by all as an able and talented military leader. General William T. Sherman thought that General Crook was the greatest Indian fighter in the West and the best the Army ever had. He grew up on a farm in Ohio and was a graduate of West Point, finishing in the bottom half of his class.

After serving in Ohio and on the west coast, he was sent to Arizona by President Ulysses S. Grantm and was placed in command of the Department of Arizona in 1871. His number one enemy was the Apaches. By 1873 he was famous for using Indian scouts and fought the Indians only when he had to and relative peace reigned in the Arizona territories. The Indians were on reservations but it was a peace that was eventually broken. He never did conquer the Apaches but was a compassionate man who made sure that his command did not use excess in punishing the Indians. Although Chief Red Cloud had fought against him, he was friendly to the General. Upon the death of the general, Chief Red Cloud said: "He never lied to us. His words gave the people hope." Many called him the "terrible and the just." He never used profanity which made him something special among his troops.

General Crook left the Gila country in 1886. After years

of Indian fighting, he defined his position by saying:

> It should not be expected that an Indian who has lived as a barbarian all his life will become an angel the moment he comes on a reservation and promises to behave himself. Or that he has that strict sense of honor that a person should have who has had the advantage of civilization all his life, and the benefit of a moral training and character which has been transmitted to him through a long line of ancestors. It requires constant watching and knowledge of their character to keep them from going wrong. They are children in ignorance not in innocence. I do not wish to be understood as in the least palliating their crimes, but I wish to say a word to stem the torrent of invective and abuse which has and had been indulged in against the whole Apache race.
>
> I have no knowledge of a case on record where a white man has been convicted and punished for defrauding an Indian. Greed and avarice on the part of the whites . . . in other words the almighty dollar is at the bottom of nine tenths of all our Indian trouble.

The Gila, River of the Southwest by Edwin Corle, page 305.

Winnie Ruth Judd

In the history of Arizona many murders were committed. Probably the most famous murderer was a lady by the name of Winnie Ruth Judd. On October 16, 1931, in Phoenix she killed two of her best friends. One of the bodies was hacked to pieces. Both bodies were then put in a trunk and shipped to Los Angeles. They were found three days later. Judd was sentenced to death in 1932. She pleaded insanity. Her trial was the talk of the nation. She was freed in 1971 and moved to San Francisco. She died in Phoenix in October of 1998. Many of her friends feel today that she was not guilty and that she acted in self defense. In this point of time, only God knows the answers.

John Charles Fremont

This is the story of a man who almost became President of the United States in 1856 as a Republican, but lost the election. He also gained fame in the war with Mexico by winning a huge battle at Rancho Cahuenga in 1847 which, in fact, stopped the Mexicans from overrunning California. He was later convicted of insubordination to a superior officer and was to be dismissed from the Army. However, this never happened as his father-in-law, Thomas H. Benton, a powerful U.S. senator, used his influence to stop the proceedings.

While living in New York Fremont and his family had limited financial means and were forced to live on a small military pension and the writings of his wife, Jessie. They eventually got in contact with Fremont's good friend and admirer, President Rutherford Hayes, who appointed him to the governorship of Arizona. He then moved his family to Prescott, Arizona. This position was a boost to his morale. But like in all his previous notable adventures, he was to fail in this one too. He became very interested in gold and silver mining and sought investors by going often to New York. His lack of interest in Arizona administrative affairs did not go unnoticed in Arizona and in Washington. Chester Arthur, then in the White House, recalled him in 1881. His gold mining endeavors never worked out and with a deep sense of frustration, he and his family moved back to New York. He led a humble life with very little financial security and died in 1890. His wife, Jessie, passed away in 1902.

Chapter Eighteen

THE BLACK MAN IN ARIZONA

There comes a time when the cup of endurance runs over, and men are no longer willing to be plunged into an abyss of injustice where they experience the bleakness of corroding despair. I hope, sirs, you can understand our legitimate and unavoidable impatience.

Martin Luther King, Jr.

If one is to write a history of Arizona, some mention should be made of the great contributions of the black man. Very few books on Arizona history have made any real reference to these great people. We shall attempt to peruse some of their significant contributions.

The first black man mentioned in Arizona history has to be the black slave, Estevan or Etevanico. By religion he was a Moslem. He departed Culican, Mexico, on March 7, 1539, with the famous Father Marcos De Niza, a Franciscan missionary. They are famous in history for their expedition to find the famed seven gold cities of Cibola.

Many of the forty-niners going to California in the big gold strike of 1849 were black men. Many believed that they

189

had a sixth sense for finding gold and they were welcomed by most white men.

Arizona had many black cowboys. Between 1870 and 1900, black cowboys made a big impact on our history but few history books record this information. Black ranch hands constituted nearly one fourth of the work force of the West.

John Swain, a famous black cowboy, died in Tombstone, Arizona, in 1945 at the age of ninety-nine. Employed by John Slaughter for many years, Swain gained a reputation as the right hand man for Slaughter as he built his cattle empires in New Mexico and Texas. He is buried in Tombstone in the famous Boothill Cemetery.

The blacks played a big role in the military history of Arizona and, for that matter, throughout the West. They were known as Buffalo soldiers, so nicknamed by the Indians in respect to the sacred animal. Also the blacks had wooly hair and it was likened to the buffalo mane.

The blacks served with distinction in the West. Altogether, they comprised about fifteen percent of the military in the West in the approximately fifty years after the Civil War.

The author had the privilege of talking with Sergeant John Campbell in his home in Phoenix. He is the last Buffalo soldier alive at that time who served at Fort Huachuca, arriving there in 1912. He pointed out that the Indians in our history were very fond of the black soldier. Fort Huachuca was a good duty post and the summers were not too hot because of the higher elevation in that area. He is proud of the thirty-three years he served in the Army and states that he was treated very well by the command structure.

The blacks fought usually in all black outfits. Officially both the 9th and 10th U.S. Cavalry were created out of a Federal Act of July, 1866. It determined that "to the regiments of Cavalry now in service shall be added four regiments, two of which shall be composed of colored men." At Jefferson Barracks in Missouri, Lt. Col. Benjamin Gierson, a former music teacher, who was a former war hero for the North, was the first commander of the 10th Cavalry. In New Orleans the 9th Cavalry was organized by Col. Edward Hatch.

Among the commissioned officers of the 10th Cavalry in their glorious history was Lt. John J. Pershing, who later was to lead the U.S. Army in World War I. Also, Col. Leonard Wood served with these fine soldiers. He was to become eventually the Chief of Staff during World War I. Only two black officers were to serve these units in Arizona covering a period of some fifty years. They were Henry O. Flipper and Charles Young, both graduates of West Point Military Academy.

During the 1920s and 1930s blacks migrated to new settlements around the state of Arizona. Blacks around Tucson attempted a mining venture in 1912, led by J.W. Miller. It was to prove to be unsuccessful.

A memorable event in the history of Phoenix was the celebrated visit by Booker T. Washington. He was guest speaker at the Emancipation Proclamation celebration, commemorated on October 23 and 24, 1911.

The school system for years in Arizona had separate schools for the whites and the blacks. Tucson's first Jim Crow School was opened when the city had fourteen black families. The first classes were in a small house at Sixth Street and Sixth Avenue. Phoenix Union Colored High School was organized in 1922. In 1926 the school moved into an adequate building at 415 East Grant that was to house it until 1953.

The Klu Klux Klan paraded in Phoenix in the 1920s and was very active. It often visited white and black churches. While visiting the blacks, they would put money in the collection plate. They left the message loud and clear that they would support the black community, as long "as they remained in their place." The stigma of discrimination was accelerated more after Arizona became a state. In territorial days, the blacks were more accepted in the white community. Statehood brought in more Southerners with deeper dislike for the blacks.

The author visited the separate black grade school in Nogales, Arizona, in 1950. He was warmly received many times by the genial and competent black faculty. But it was apparent that in Nogales, as well as in other parts of the state, the blacks did not have equal buildings or grounds in comparison to their white brethren. Carver High School in Phoenix for a long time felt this burden.

Phoenix Union High School District took action on desegregation a year prior to the United States Supreme Court decision of 1954.

Two black families who came to Phoenix around the turn of the century were the Crumps and the Rossers. Both families settled in the predominantly black East Jefferson Street. Both families still live in Phoenix.

Miss Irene Rosser lived on East Jefferson and was the surviving daughter of Mr. and Mrs. Richard Rosser who migrated from Georgia with a large family. In a personal chat at her home, Miss Rosser gave the author the interesting experience of interviewing her and discussing the early days in Phoenix. She remembered early Phoenix well. Just about everyone slept outside in the summertime. An iceman brought the ice each day to the homes. The food was more nutritious than it is today, and people had more fun in the 1900s than they do today. Hay rides and barbecues were the big events. There was running water in the homes and the blacks were very few. Miss Rosser did not mind the heat without air conditioning but the dust storms were absolutely ferocious.

The National Association for the Advancement of Colored People came into Phoenix in the 1940s. The Urban League founded a branch office in Phoenix in 1945.

During the 1960s, when the rest of the nation was pushing civil rights and there was civil rebellion in the land, Arizona assumed its maturity and passed a Public Accommodation ordinance as well as a civil rights package.

All in all, blacks have made their mark in the history of Arizona. They number about 95,000 in the state today. To say that there is no discrimination in Arizona today is not true.

In the general election of 1990, Arizona failed to pass legislation to enact a paid holiday to honor Martin Luther King, Jr. Since it was one of the few states in the nation that did not have such a day, Arizona quickly received the reputation on a national scale that it was racist. The so-called reputation was not true, for Arizona was not a racist state. Like all states we had people who had extremist views against civil rights and we had many who favored civil rights.

In 1992 in the general election, the people of Arizona voted for a paid holiday for state employees and a state holiday to honor Dr. King.

Chapter Nineteen

ARIZONA TERRITORIAL PRISON IN YUMA

In Yuma is the Territorial Prison, which is now partly completed, and when fully finished according to the plans and specifications, will be a model of strength, utility and architectural beauty. Among the other important buildings are the country courthouse, jail, public schoolhouse, Catholic school, two hotels, printing office, private dwellings, and a large number of fine stores and saloons. The Sentinel is a wide awake newspaper, is well established at Yuma, and thoroughly devoted to the interests of the country and territory.

> Hiram C. Hodge
> *Arizona, As it is*, 1877.

  The Yuma Territorial Prison is located in Yuma, Arizona. It was in operation for thirty-three* years from 1876 to 1909. Eventually it was called the "Hell Hole," a name that was first used by the Ft. Yuma soldiers because of the heat in Yuma, and eventually the nickname extended to the prison. Described as a desert Alcatraz, it had some of the roughest and toughest characters the West has ever known.

*The facts in this chapter have been checked by Jo Masterson and Reba Grandrud, Historian, of the Yuma Territorial Prison State Historical Park. Their recommended corrections have been added to this revised chapter.

194

Arizona had so many criminals during the 1870s and 1880s that the town jail could not secure all the prisoners without a few escaping. Officers of the law were pretty good, so many arrests and convictions are evident. For this reason, a prison was needed badly in Arizona. During 1875, the prison was authorized by the legislature of Yuma. The cost of the prison was to be $25,000 and completion of the prison was accomplished by the inmates.

The prison is located at the top of a gravel road called Prison Hill. Looking off in the distance you can see the Colorado River which has narrowed in width since the building of man-made obstacles. Looking off to the north it is possible to see the Gila River which was turbulent and unpredictable during flood season.

Location of the Territorial Prison at Yuma was a legislative feat of the 1875 session, in which Jose Redondo played a leading part. He came to be known as the "father of the penitentiary." The competition of numerous towns, principally Prescott, Florence, and Phoenix to secure the prison had apparently been settled by the legislature of 1873, through the passage of a bill naming Phoenix as the site. However, no funds for construction were provided, as it was expected that the cost would be met by the federal government. Thereby Phoenix lost its opportunity to become a penal colony instead of the capital city. The Yuma strategists under the leadership of Councilman Redondo and Representative R.D. Kelly had the bill amended to read "Yuma". When the measure passed Redondo was chosen by joint vote of the two houses as a member of the Board of Prison commissioners. The other members were David Neahf of Yuma and William H. Hardy of Mohave County.

The act establishing the prison at Yuma provided for a bond issue of $25,000 bearing ten percent interest and payable in five years. In November 1874, the commission sold the bonds to A. Luther, of San Francisco, the only bidder, for about $19,000.

Al Grow submitted plans for the prison and was paid $150. With the building funds a plant was constructed consisting of adobe walls five-and-one-half feet thick at the base, built on a solid rock foundation; two stone cells, an adobe building containing two prison rooms estimated to have a capacity of thirty prisoners, a kitchen, dining room, hall room for guards, superintendent's quarters, a water reservoir, boiler and engine and a well-equipped blacksmith shop.

In his message to the 1877 Legislature, Governor Safford acknowledged that the commissioners had performed their duties faithfully and well. "The whole work," he said, "seems to have been done in the most substantial manner and the prison is considered by those who have examined it as secure a place for the confinement of prisoners as can be found in most of the older states." He was also pleased to be able to state, "that the money appropriated for the construction of the prison had been expended in an economical manner," and considered that the "thanks of the people are due to the Commissioners for their services, which they have given without pecuniary reward."

The Arizona Territorial Penitentiary was a model for cleanliness. Most of the prisoners took some pride in keeping it that way. This fact, no doubt, tended to raise the morale of the convicts. It is said that if a prisoner was careless about bathing, he was sent to the Dark Cell.

Well-cooked, wholesome meals were prepared in the prison kitchen and served in the immaculately clean dining room. The prisoners worked rather hard all day and they were kept better satisfied with good food.

The prison buildings were squat. They have decayed quite a bit since its closing. The prison looks like a medieval fortress. On all corners of the prison walls were guard towers, manned by rifle men who commanded every foot of the enclosed prison walls. The inside of the prison consisted of the main cell blocks, prisoners mess hall, exercise yard, blacksmith shop, bull pen, recreation hall for Sundays, women's ward, and tuberculosis ward.

On the north side of the prison is the "sally port" which means entryway. There also is the mess hall, the stables, the arsenal, superintendent's cottage and the main guard tower.

Every one of the cells in stunted. The cells are seven feet wide by nine feet deep and thirteen feet high to the arch in the cell. Inside the cells are two tiers of bunks, three bunks to each tier, made of steel, each bunk just eighteen inches wide. There was no washbowl or any type of furniture and no toilet facilities, except a galvanized bucket which was emptied but once a day and served six inmates, if the cell was full.

In the months of May through September the heat comes to Yuma. Sometimes the temperatures would soar as high as 120 degrees in the shade. At night the town people slept on the porches with dampened sheets to get some measure of comfort. Inside the prison, because of the thick walls, the temperature was ten to twelve degrees cooler in the summer. A sixty inch fan circulated the air in the cell block. In the winter, the temperature was ten to twelve degrees warmer on the inside of the prison. During the winter, the electrical plant on the east side of the cellblock helped heat the cells. The prisoners had one blanket, a skimpy straw tick for a mattress. Sickness was prevalent with colds quickly developing into pneumonia. There was quite a bit of tuberculosis during this period of time and most evident in the Indian prisoners.

For the prisoners who disobeyed while in prison, they were sent to a place called the dungeon or "snake den" or Dark Cell, as called by the guards. The last Dark Cell is fifteen feet by fifteen feet with a strap iron cage eight feet by ten feet by five feet high. There the prisoners lived on bread and water. The cell was blasted out of solid rock. A narrow passageway defined the entrance, with the cell being in complete darkness, except when the sun was directly overhead. There was minimal ventilation. This was a place to test a man's soul. Ten days was about the limit a man could stand in the "snake den". The prisoners had no bed except the bare ground to sleep on. He was kept shackled. There was not even blankets or a mattress for some comfort. There were no sanitary conditions. The prisoner usually used one corner of the floor. There was no contact with the outside world except for the daily ration.

What would break a man's spirit was the fact that he could be terrorized by scorpions and snakes. Some of the prisoners swore that some of the sadistic guards threw poisonous things inside the cell to further torture the prisoner. When the press heard of this, the prison officials denied it. They said that these things either crawled into the passageway or fell in through the ventilator. Prison officials have stated that any guard caught mistreating a prisoner was fired.

There was another type of cell, cut out of the same solid rock. This type of cell was known as the crazy hole. The cell was about five feet by four with just hardly enough headroom for a man who is tall. It was for insane prisoners. They threw the individual in there until he was transferred to the Phoenix Asylum. It would probably drive even a rational man crazy, let alone an insane man.

The prisoners on good behavior, were occasionally entertained by town people. Some music and singing was the usual form and was very much appreciated by the men. This took away some of the men's pressures.

Efforts were made by the superintendents to keep the prisoner occupied without relaxing any of the strict discipline. Many of the men on good behavior were employed with various jobs. Some were employed in the blacksmith shop, around the stables, in the mattress factory, tailor shop, mess hall, and in various other jobs. Trustees of the prison were relieved of some of the hard work and they also had the run of the inner yards.

All the convicts who were able-bodied worked while in

the prison, according to Rules and Regulations 29. They had it really tough. They probably wished they had died a thousand times before they were through with their sentence. They had to break rocks all day. They also made adobes which were not only used for new prison construction, but were sold to the township for their own use. This type labor for prisoners meant long hours in the almost unbearable summer heat. Many men collapsed from sheer exhaustion. Others were struck down by sunstroke, some dying.

One of the most interesting sites upon entering the Yuma Territorial Prison was the guard tower, located north and east of the prison wall. The structure was high, with open sides and a sloping roof. It is reminiscent of a bandstand in the earlier era when on Sunday afternoon, concerts were the order of the day. By far, this was no concert for the prisoners. During jail break the noise of rifle bullets from its catwalks, the chattering of the huge Lowell Battery gun from the platform, were certainly no type of music to the ears of the desperate men trying to escape.

The weapon known as the Lowell Battery gun, could fire 300 rounds per minute operated by one person and 600 rounds per minute operated by two persons. This was a forerunner to the modern machine gun. The gun was mounted on a two wheel carriage for rapid maneuvering, and it was manned by two men who knew how to operate it. The tower in which the gun was located, was under the ever-watchful guards who commanded and had a visual sweep in all directions.

The science of penology, practiced Arizona style, circa 1875, was not very advanced. Prisoners with tuberculosis were put in a separate TC cell. Insane prisoners were put in an insane cell. Those who misbehaved were put in the "dungeon". Prisoners who died there were buried in the prison cemetery. The graves of 104 unfortunate beings may be seen today at the prison. Eleven died of natural causes and ten prisoners died while trying to escape.

A total of twenty-six prisoners escaped from the prison. Of these, two escaped from inside the prison, and four went down river to Mexico and ended up in the Mexican Revolutionary Army. The desert all around was invisible but almost an unassailable wall.

Among those present at Yuma was Buckskin Frank Leslie, scout, marksman and Indian fighter and all-around Tombstone character. Once at the Bird Cage Theatre, watching a performance from the orchestra, Buckskin Frank waxed wrath over a drunken cowboy sprawled in an upper box with his feet on the rail. In the middle of the show he drew his six-gun and shot the heel of the cowboy's boot, which persuaded the cowboy thereafter to keep his feet where they belonged. It was not for this, though, that Buckskin Frank was sent to Yuma but for shooting his common law wife, Mollie. He received a life sentence. He worked in the prison hospital with the TB prisoners and because he put his life in danger, he was paroled early.

Throughout the history of the prison there were about 29 women inmates. Among these was Pearl Hart, stage robber. Pearl originally flirted with the jury and got off on the stagecoach robbery charge. The judge was so upset he had her charged with possession of the pistol of the stagecoach driver. She got five years. So far as anybody knows, that was the only crime Pearl ever committed, but she made an awfully good thing of it. She was written up in a New York newspaper and a national magazine and eventually went into vaudeville. There she exploited audiences with hairy and largely fictitious accounts of her criminal escapades in the terrible Yuma prison.

Pearl was much less formidable, really, than two others of Yuma's female prisoners. One was a belle of casual virtue known as Lizzie. Although it wasn't the easiest thing in the world to find grounds upon which to insult Lizzie, a soldier managed to do so during a dance in Yuma. Lizzie thereupon stabbed the soldier, receiving in return from the Territory of

Arizona, a 15-month sentence in the Yuma Prison. She had languished therein for only a few months, however, when a man came along who operated a traveling saloon on the railroad. He took a shine to Liz and talked the authorities into allowing them to wed. That done, the prison board gave Liz a pardon, and she and her itinerant gallant left and were never seen again.

Surely the toughest of them all, though, was Elena Estrada, a Latin spitfire with what impressionable journalists of the period were pleased to describe as "cat's eyes". But it wasn't her eyes that made Elana famous. It was her passion for thoroughness. She was in the Yuma prison for having killed her man. She said at the trial that he fell on her knife repeatedly. The hole in his chest was large enough to have removed the heart (and legend said that she had removed his heart and slapped him with it!). However, his heart was still in his chest according to the doctor's report.

The story of the prison is complicated since the rules changed with each superintendent. One write-up, by a visitor, tells of the prisoners entering the mess hall unchained and conversing as "travelers at a wayside inn".

Another write-up gives a different picture. The prisoners were chained in groups of five or six, and no conversations were allowed at any time in the mess hall. It is generally agreed that the prisoners were well treated and the prison was a model institution of its day.

Of course, the cruel and sadistic angle is always played up by writers and much of the good treatment is ignored. It is possible and probably true that individual guards were cruel; but then, this condition exists in many penal institutions today.

Other stories vary too. There are four published versions of a riot in which Mrs. Charles Ingalls, wife of the superintendent, played a part. All vary, some with great stretch of the imagination. However, prison records indicate that Mrs. Ingalls was well-liked by the prisoners, as she started the first library in

Yuma at the prison so that prisoners who wished to learn to read and write could do so. Other stories are written with an eye to giving the public an exciting story—factual or not.

The following is a complete and accurate list of the superintendents of the Territorial Prison at Yuma. The last territorial superintendent was appointed in 1907, and the last prisoners were moved to Florence in April, 1909. A letter from Thomas Rynning shows that 180 short-term prisoners and 18 long-term prisoners were moved to Florence at that time.

> 1875—William A. Werninger, Sheriff of Yuma Co.
> Appointed Supt. of Territorial prisoners confined in Yuma jail until completion of prison.
> Son-in-law of Jose Redondo.
> 1876—Geo. M. Thurlow (June 22nd). Resigned Jan. 11, 1881.
> 1881—C.V. Meeden (Jan. 11th) to fill unexpired term.
> 1883—F.S. Ingalls (June 12th)
> 1886—Thomas Gates (July 16th)
> 1888—John H. Behan (Apr. 12th)
> 1890—F.S. Ingalls (Apr. 7th)
> 1891—M. M. McInernay (Sept. 3rd)
> 1893—Wm. K. Meade (Apr. 24th)
> 1893—Thomas Gates (July 13th)
> 1896—Mike J. Nugent (July 14th)
> 1897—John W. Dorrington (July 31st)
> 1898—Herbert Brown (Sept. 10th)
> 1902—Wm. M. Griffith (June 4th)
> 1904—R.F. Daniels (Oct. 3rd)
> 1905—Jerry Millay (June 5th)
> 1907—Thos. Rynning (Jan. 4th)

After the prison closed in 1909, the building became the location for classes held by Yuma High School. . Because of the school's origin, "Criminals" became the nickname of the student body.

It must be noted here however, that many of the stories about the prison have been exaggerated beyond the bounds of truth. There is a school of thought among historians who will say that the prison was a model institution and it was one of the better ones in the West. Too many writers have tried to exploit its history to make it appear as a "Hell Hole". Needless to say, it was not a pleasant place to be sent to, but, on the other hand, it was a good prison for its time.

Chapter Twenty

ARIZONA KALEIDOSCOPE

I even heard the complaint made that the thermometer failed to show the true heat because the mercury dried up. Everything dries; wagons, men dry; chickens dry, there is no juice left in anything, living or dead, by the close of the summer in Yuma. Chickens hatched at this season, as old fort Yumers say, come out of the shell ready cooked.

J. Ross Browne,
Adventures in Apache Country, 1864

SPANISH PERIOD—1528-1821

1528-36	Odyssey of Cabeza de Vaca stimulates desire to explore northern frontier of Mexico.
1539	Fray Marcos de Niza plods northward from Mexico.
1540-42	Francisco Vasquez de Coronado leads grand expedition to Arizona, New Mexico, and Kansas; white men first see Grand Canyon.
1582-83	Antonio de Espejo leads mining exploration up Rio Grande into New Mexico, then westward into Arizona.
1589-1607	Juan de Onate's party explores northern Arizona to Gulf of California.
1600	Franciscan missionaries attempted conversion of Indians in New Mexico and northeastern Arizona.
1608	City of Santa Fe founded by Pedro de Peralta.
1680	Pueblo revolt strikes Spanish culture on northern frontier.

204

1696	Father Eusebio Francisco Kino brings Christianity to Indians of Pimeria Alta.
1696	Mission of Tumacacori established.
1700	Father Kino lays foundation of first Mission of San Xavier del Bac.
1736	Miraculous silver discovery (planchas de plata) in Arizona.
1751	Pimeria uprising against Spanish officials and priests.
1752	Presidio at Tubac established to subdue Indian revolt.
1767	King Carlos III expels Jesuits from Spanish realm.
1768	Father Francisco Garces takes charge at San Xavier as Franciscans are assigned to Arizona.
1774	Garces accompanies Anza on expedition to find route from Sonora to the western sea.
1775-1776	Second Anza-Garces expedition; Garces travels widely in Arizona.
1776	Presidio garrison moved from Tubac to Tucson; Spain adopts new plan for controlling northern frontier.
1785-1810	Yuma Massacre blights Spanish settlement in Arizona; Garces martyred.
1785-1810	Apaches pacified by bribes; prosperity in Pimeria Alta.
1810-1821	Northern provinces neglected as Spanish colonies in New World revolt.

MEXICAN PERIOD—1821-1848

1821	Santa Fe trade route opened. Spanish expelled from Mexico. Mexico became independent country.
1823	First Texas settlements by Americans. Wagons of the Santa Fe trade reach Arizona.
1824-1840	American mountainmen trap along Arizona streams for beaver and find traces of placer gold.
1830s	Scalp hunters roam Southwest to earn bounty payments offered in Mexico for Apache scalps.
1846	Mexican War brings Army of the West through Central Arizona; Kearny proclaims sovereignty of the United States in area; Cooke leads Mormon

	Battalion across southern Arizona, marking out army wagon road.
1848	Treaty of Guadalupe Hidalgo pledges United States to pacify boundary along Gila River and Rio Grande, marking vast Mexican cession.

AMERICAN PERIOD—1848-1999

1848	Treaty of Guadalupe Hidalgo brings huge undeveloped area into United States.
1849	Gold seekers use Cooke's Wagon Road in rush to California diggings.
1850	Compromise Act of 1850 establishes Territory of New Mexico, which includes Arizona north of the Gila River.
1850-1851	Boundary commission under John Russell Bartlett surveys new international boundary from Rio Grande to Colorado River.
1851	Fort Defiance established in northeastern corner of Arizona.
1852	Fort Yuma on California shore of Colorado protects river crossing. Captain Lorenzo Sitgreaves leads exploring expedition along 35th parallel, then to Fort Yuma. Uncle Sam, first steamboat on Colorado.
1853	Gadsden Purchase brings United States land south of Gila extending into southern New Mexico.
1853-1854	Lieutenant A.W. Whipple makes railroad survey along 35th parallel
1854	Charles D. Poston and Herman Ehrenberg arrive in Arizona, finding interesting mining prospects.
1855	Lieutenant William H. Emory surveys international boundary extended by Gadsden Purchase.
1856	Mexican garrison leaves Tucson; U.S. Dragoons arrive. American residents of Arizona petition Congress for separation from New Mexico.
1857	Fort Buchanan established in southern Arizona.
1857-1858	Lieutenant Edward F. Beale surveys wagon route on 35th parallel, using camels as pack animals.
1858	Butterfield Overland Stage begins operation across Arizona.
1859	Fort Mohave established on Colorado River in

	northwestern Arizona.
1861	Bascom Affair inflames Chiricahua Apaches; withdrawal of troops at outbreak of Civil War encourages Indian raiding; Arizona declares itself Confederate in bid for protection.
1862	Jefferson Davis on February 14 declares Arizona a territory of the Confederate States of America. Skirmish at Picacho Pass is only significant Civil War encounter between Confederate and Union troops in Arizona; James H. Carleton leads Califor nia Column across desert, reestablishing it as United States territory; fierce battle fought at Apache Pass between Union troops and combined Apache force under Mangas Colorado and Cochise; Fort Bowie established to guard Apache Pass.
1863	On February 24 President Lincoln signs law creat ing Territory of Arizona; government party sworn into office at Navajo Springs late in December. Walker party prospects for gold in mountains near Prescott. Navajos ordered confined to reservation at Bosque Redondo, New Mexico.
1864	Capital moved from Chino alley to new town called Prescott; First Territorial Legislature meets, September 26-December 10; counties of Yuma, Mohave, Yavapai and Pima created; population 4,573, does not include Indians.
1866-1886	Army posts and Indian reservations provide profit-able market for beef.
1867	Territorial capital moved to Tucson.
1869-1877	Governor Anson P.K. Safford crusades for public school system.
1869	John Wesley Powell leads party exploring Colorado River canyons.
1871	Camp Grant Massacre horrifies nation; President Grant institutes peace policy in Arizona.
1872	General George Crook embarks upon military conquest of northern Apaches.
1873	Northern Apaches concentrated on San Carlos Indian Reservation.
1875	First major copper production in Arizona.
1877	Rich mineralized ledges discovered at Bisbee; Ed

	Scheiffelin finds silver bonanza which makes Tombstone famous boomtown.
	Southern Pacific railroad reaches Fort Yuma from the west; territorial prison opened on bluff beside Colorado River.
	Territorial capital returned to Prescott.
1880	Southern Pacific completes line across Arizona to New Mexico.
1881	Atlantic and Pacific (later the Santa Fe) reaches Winslow, Arizona, building westward.
1882	Outbreaks from reservation; major military operations against Apaches.
1885	Legislature appropriates first funds for higher education, authorizing university and normal school.
1886	Geronimo and renegade Chiricahua Apaches captured and exiled to Florida, ending Indian wars in Arizona.
	Higher education started with opening of Arizona Territorial Normal School at Tempe.
1888	Copper replaces gold and silver in economic importance in Arizona.
1889	Capital makes final, permanent move to Phoenix.
1891	University of Arizona holds first classes.
1893	Demonetization of silver hurts Arizona mining industry.
1899	Northern Arizona Normal School at Flagstaff established.
1901	Grand Canyon connected to Santa Fe Railroad by spur line.
1902	Plan for joint statehood of Arizona and New Mexico causes several years of quarreling.
1903	Salt River Valley Water Users' Association formed; becomes model for other irrigation districts in nation.
1907	Gambling prohibited in Arizona.
1910	Arizona Enabling Act passed by Congress; Constitutional Convention meets.
1911	Theodore Roosevelt dedicates completed Tonto (Roosevelt) Dam on Salt River.
	President Taft vetoes admission of Arizona in opposition to recall of judges; Arizona agrees to make

	the change demanded by President; first election of statehood officials.
1912	Arizona admitted to Union as 48th state on February 14; within nine months recall of judges restored to constitution.
	Plank highway built across sand dunes west of Yuma.
1917	Nation's first municipal airport established at Tucson.
	Mining boom in Arizona threatened by strike fostered by I.W.W. ; Bisbee Deportation causes national stir.
1919	Grand Canyon becomes national park.
1926	First scheduled commercial air service in Arizona.
1928	Coolidge Dam completed and dedicated by President Calvin Coolidge.
1930	The planet Pluto discovered at Lowell Observatory, Flagstaff.
1936	President Franklin D. Roosevelt dedicates Boulder Dam, later to be renamed Hoover Dam.
1941	Clouds of war bring increased military operations to Arizona.
1946	American Institute for Foreign Trade established at closed air training field near Glendale.
	Arizona right-to-work law becomes effective; industrial development and manufacturing take on new importance.
1953	Closing of United Verde Extension Mine marks end of fabulous mining span at Jerome, Arizona.
1963	Arizona wins United States Supreme Court decision in long contest for share of Colorado River water; hope revived that Central Arizona Project can be achieved.
1964	Senator Barry Goldwater, Republican Party nominee for President.
1968	Enactment of Colorado Basin Act authorized construction of Central Arizona Project.
	Senator Carl Hayden retired after representing Arizona in the House and the Senate since 1912.
1971	Jack Williams . . . began serving first four year term as governor.
1973	Vietnam . . . Prisoners of war return to Arizona.

1975	Raul H. Castro . . . inaugurated as the first Mexican American governor.
1977	Wesley Bolin becomes governor of Arizona.
1978	Bruce Babbitt becomes governor of Arizona.
1980	Senator Barry Goldwater reelected to the United States Senate.
1981	Justice Sandra O'Connor from Arizona becomes first woman appointed to U.S. Supreme Court.
1982	Because of the increase of population, Arizona will add a new Congressman.
1981	Palo Verde Nuclear Plant, 50 miles west of Phoenix nears completion. Is world's largest nuclear plant.
1985	Oscar Palmer inventor and philanthropist dies.
1986	William H. Rehnquist of Phoenix appointed Chief Justice of the U.S. Supreme Court.
1986	Sun City Vistoso begins to be built in Tucson. It is the third active adult community to be built by Del Webb Communities, Inc.
1987	Arizona State University football team selected to represent PAC Ten in Ten Rose Bowl, January 1, 1987. Defeats the University of Michigan 22-15.
1987	Frank X. Gordon Jr., first person of Polish descent to become chief justice of Arizona Supreme Court.
1987	Pope John Paul visits Phoenix.
1988	Governor Evan Mecham impeached.
1998	Arizona Diamondbacks baseball team begins first season.
	Senator Barry Goldwater died.
	Congressman Morris Udall died.

Chapter Twenty-One

ARIZONA STATISTICS

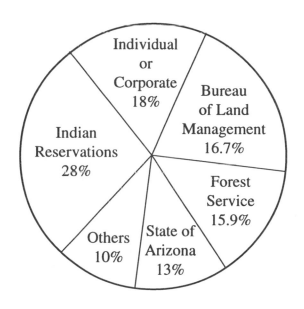

ARIZONA'S
LAND OWNERSHIP

Arizona's Governors

Territorial

John N. Goodwin	1863-66	Nathan O. Murphy	1892-93
Richard C. McCormick	1866-69	Louis C. Hughes	1893-96
A.P.K. Safford	1869-77	Bengamin J. Franklin	1896-97
John P. Hoyt	1877-78	Myron H. McCord	1897-98
John C. Fremont	1878-81	Nathan O. Murphy	1898-02
Frederick Tritle	1881-85	Alexander O. Brodie	1902-09
C. Meyer Zulich	1885-89	Joseph H. Kibby	1905-09
Lewis Wolfrey	1889-90	Richard E. Sloan	1909-12
John N. Irwin	1890-92		

State

George W. P. Hunt	1912-17	J. Howard Pyle	1951-55
Thomas E. Campbell	1917-17	Ernest W. McFarland	1955-59
George W. P. Hunt	1917-19	Paul Fannin	1959-65
Thomas E. Campbell	1919-23	Sam P. Goddard	1965-67
George W. P. Hunt	1923-29	John R. Williams	1967-75
John C. Phillips	1929-31	Raul Castro	1975-77
George W. P. Hunt	1931-33	Wesley Bolin	1977-78
Benjamin Moeur	1933-37	Bruce Babbitt	1978-86
R. C. Stanford	1937-39	Evan Mecham	1986-88
R. T. Jones	1939-41	Rose Mofford	1988-91
Sidney P. Osborn	1941-48	J. Fife Symington III	1991-97
Dan E. Garey	1949-51	Jane Hull	1997-

Members in Congress

Senators

Henry F. Ashurst	1912-41
Marcus A. Smith	1912-21
Ralph H. Cameron	1921-27
Carl Hayden	1927-69
Earnest W. McFarland	1941-53
Barry Goldwater	1953-86
Paul Fannin	1965-77
Dennis DeConcini	1977-94
John McCain	1986-
John Kyle	1994-

Representatives

Carl Hayden	1912-27
Lewis W. Douglas	1927-33
Mrs. Isabella Greenway	1933-37
John R. Murdock	1937-43
Richard Harless	1943-49
Harold A. Patten	1949-53
Stewart Udall	1955-60
John Rhodes	1953-82
Morris Udall	1955-60
George F. Senner, Jr.	1963-67
Sam Steiger	1967-77
John Conlan	1973-77
Eldon Rudd	1977-86
Robert Stump	1977-
Jim Kolbe	1985-
Jon Kyl	1986-94
Jay Rhodes	1986-92
Ed Pastor	1991-
Matt Selman	1994-
John Shadegg	1994-
J. D. Hayworth	1994-
John McCain	1982-1986

Chapter Twenty-Two

EPILOGUE

Let us look at Arizona as it is today and as it will be in the twenty-first century.

With the coming of the twenty-first century, it is apparent that women will play a bigger role in the economic and social life of this country. In the Arizona election of 1998 five women were elected to the most powerful, elected offices. Governor Jane Hull was elected Governor, Betsey Bayless the new Secretary of State, Janet Napolitano the office of Attorney General, Lisa Graham Keegan the Superintendent of Education and Carol Springer the State Treasurer. Arizona has ousted two Republican, male governors in eight years and that may be the real reason why the voters chose women in this election.

In looking over the picture of politics in this state, we all know that Arizona is a very, very conservative state. In recent years it has been very Republican. The majority in the state legislature are Republicans as are most of the radio and television stations. The crime rate is very high in the major cities and many citizens are pointing out that Arizona is building more prisons than schools.

Most of the land in Arizona is owned by the federal and

state governments and factoring in the twenty-one Indian reservations, this leaves only about 17 percent of the land that can be taxed. Over the years this has hampered social and educational progress. For budget reasons the universities, community colleges and the school districts love to hire part-time instructors with the proviso that they receive no benefits and no real job security. Charter schools are also very popular. Arizona has more charter schools than any state in the Union. Arizona's teachers and professors are paid poorly. Also the mental health care, along with providing for medical needs of dependent children, are wanting. Adult mental health care leaves a lot to be desired. The number of prison guards in our prisons is terribly understaffed. Funding for the construction of roads and highways is also lacking as is the financial battle to fight pollution.

To offset the many important needs for monies, Arizona is looking forward to tobacco money. The state will receive about 177 million dollars in up-front payments starting in 1999, and over five years for its part in a national settlement with the tobacco companies. After that, tobacco companies will pay to Arizona about 118 million dollars per year probably forever.

Governor Hull, a popular Republican and a former schoolteacher, has already enforced a plan whereby a new 76 million dollar mental hospital will be built. This facility is badly needed for Arizona has been lax in the care of the mentally ill.

People in the U.S. are becoming aware that Arizona is one of the best places to live. The state has an excellent climate. People can live cheaper here. Many who are ill find that this is a healthy state and many doctors in the U.S. send their patients to Arizona where the year-long sun can do wonders for many. The year 1999 will continue, hopefully, the big financial boom that we have witnessed for the past seven years and projections show the state to gain three million people in the next ten years.

Arizona soon will have a population of about eight million people but our biggest problem will be to have enough water? Water may have to be piped from the Pacific Ocean.

Arizona's voters in 1998 approved a proposition which will change the way elections are financed. The voting system presently is dominated by big money. The politician who had the most money usually won. No more. The measure will make all challengers enter the battle on a more equal, financial footing, which will lessen the power of special interests groups. This measure sends a message to the rest of the country.

Finally, Arizona has two residents who are interested in running for the White House in the year 2000. Dan Quayle, Vice President under President Bush, has already announced his desire to run. Senator John McCain also is expected to be a candidate.

Governor Jane Hull

U.S. Representative Ed Pastor

Senator John McCain;
Expected to run for the
Presidency in the year 2000

U.S. Representative
J.D. Hayworth

U.S. Representative
Shadegg

U.S. Representative
Matt Salmon

Raul Castro, Arizona's first
Hispanic governor.

Barry Goldwater and
Carol Woznicki,
the author's wife.

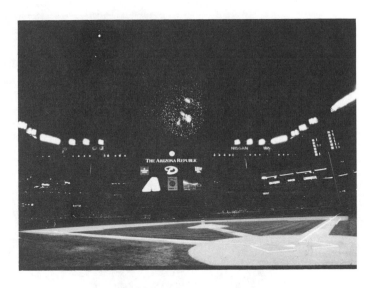

Opening Night, 1998 Arizona Diamondbacks.
Bank One Ballpark, Phoenix.
©1998 by Carl Gooding

America West Arena, home of the Phoenix Suns.

The church of San Xavier is located about 11 miles south of Tucson and it often referred to as the White Dove of the Desert. It was founded by the Jesuit Priest, Father Eusebio Francisco Kino.

The interior courtyard of San Xavier Mission is one of the newest additions to the mission. Here two altar boys await their call to early morning Mass.

Hopi Indian Reservation.

Set against the sunlit Tucson mountains, Old Tucson is a replica of early Tucson. In exchange for paving a road to the county owned site, the producers of Arizona constructed a real town of adobe and wood which attracts thousands of visitors annually.

Arizona Office of Tourism Photo.

Half a century ago, Jerome was the third largest city in Arizona. Though perilously close to it, Jerome has never really been a ghost town. At one time, the population dwindled to 20, but today Jerome's 300 residents are starting a spectacular revival.

Tombstone enjoyed a short boom as a silver mining capital from 1877 to 1886 but tales of its colorful frontier episodes have endured to the present, bolstering its reputation as "the town to tough to die."

Arizona Office of Tourism Photo.

Yuma Crossing Museum

Remnants of early days at Yuma Territorial Prison are on display near a complex built to relieve overcrowding in the main cellblock. The passageway on the right led to the main yard, dungeon, barbershop, and double row of adobe cells. The prison, which closed in 1909, was later developed into museum.

Some 200 millions years ago, Old Faithful was a living monarch of the Triassic Age forest. Today it rests peacefully in Arizona's Petrified Forest.

Arizona Office of Tourism Photo.

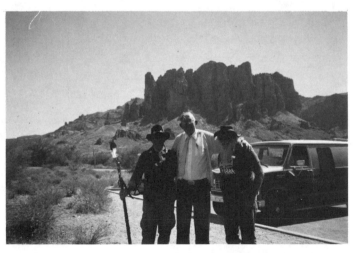

The spectacular views of the Superstition Mountains of Arizona are a major attraction for visitors and photographers. After a winter with large amounts of precipitation, this area is covered with a carpet of the most beautiful wildflowers. L-R: Ron Eagle, author, Tony Monaco.

Somewhere in the looming Superstition Mountains lies the yet un-discovered bonanza of the Lost Dutchman Gold Mine. Although visitors may not leave with a fortune in nuggets, thousands of winter visitors find instant wealth in the spectacular scenery along the Apache Trail.

Arizona Office of Tourism Photo.

INDEX

226

ARIZONA TRIVIA

1804 Pueblo of Tucson—reported by Captain Jose de Zuniga to have a population of 37 Spanish settlers and more than 200 Indians.

1847 Mormon Battalion entered California via Arizona.

1854 The Gadsen Purchase—United States obtained the region south of the Gila to the present border of Mexico.

1859 *Weekly Arizona*—First territorial newspaper printed in Tubac.

1869 Major John Wesley Powell—Made the first complete exploration of the Grand Canyon.

1912 Arizona becomes the 48th state. George Hunt is the first governor.

1917 Tenth Cavalry returned to Ford Huachuca after longest march made into Mexico during the punitive expedition against Pancho Villa.

1924 Postal Service—First parcel post package is sent airmail from Tucson to New York.

1933 Dr. Benjamin Baker Moeur inaugurated as governor. Only medical man to be Chief Executive. Known as the "Depression Governor."

1948 Arizona Indians given right to vote.

1962 Kitt Peak Observatory—World's largest solar telescope dedicated.

1975 Raul Castro inaugurated as the first Mexican American Governor of Arizona.

1998 Premier season of Bank One Ballpark, home of Arizona Diamondbacks and Arizona's first major league baseball team.
- The building contains more than 60,000 cubic yards of cast-in-place concrete.
- The roof structure weight 41.7 pounds per square foot.
- There are 340 restroom facilities for women and 276 for men.
- At peak demand, water usage will be 2,500 gallons per minute.
- The roof is opened and closed by a pair of 200-horsepower electric motors. Each time the roof is opened or closed, it runs up the electric bill just $1.